First World War
and Army of Occupation
War Diary
France, Belgium and Germany

3 CAVALRY DIVISION
Divisional Troops
Royal Army Veterinary Corps
14 Mobile Veterinary Section
3 October 1914 - 31 May 1919

WO95/1149/3

The Naval & Military Press Ltd
www.nmarchive.com
Published in association with The National Archives

Published by

The Naval & Military Press Ltd

Unit 10 Ridgewood Industrial Park,

Uckfield, East Sussex,

TN22 5QE England

Tel: +44 (0) 1825 749494

www.naval-military-press.com

www.nmarchive.com

This diary has been reprinted in facsimile from the original. Any imperfections are inevitably reproduced and the quality may fall short of modern type and cartographic standards.

© Crown Copyright
Images reproduced by permission of The National Archives, London, England, 2015.

Contents

Document type	Place/Title	Date From	Date To
Heading	WO95/1149/3		
Heading	1914-1919 3rd Cavalry Division 14th Mobile Vety Section Oct 1914-May 1919		
Heading	War Diary of 14th Mobile Vet. Section 3rd Cavalry Division October-December 1914 May 1919		
Heading	3rd Cavalry Division 14th Mobile Vety Lection Vol I		
War Diary	Woolwich	03/10/1914	04/10/1914
War Diary	Portsmouth	04/10/1914	04/10/1914
War Diary	S'Hampton	04/10/1914	11/10/1914
War Diary	Bruges	11/10/1914	12/10/1914
War Diary	Gastrelles	12/10/1914	12/10/1914
War Diary	Foures	13/10/1914	13/10/1914
War Diary	Dunkirque	14/10/1914	20/10/1914
War Diary	Boulogne	21/10/1914	22/10/1914
War Diary	Castre	23/10/1914	23/10/1914
War Diary	Ypres	24/10/1914	24/10/1914
War Diary	Zeelebeke	25/10/1914	04/11/1914
War Diary	Vlamertinghe Ypres	04/11/1914	21/11/1914
War Diary	Strazeele	21/11/1914	21/11/1914
War Diary	Hazebrouk	22/11/1914	27/11/1914
War Diary	Hondeghem	22/11/1914	27/11/1914
War Diary	Hondghem	01/12/1914	30/12/1914
Heading	War Diary of 14th Mobile Vet Section 3rd Cavalry Division Jan Feb 1915		
War Diary	Hondghem	04/01/1915	29/01/1915
War Diary	Hondeghem	01/02/1915	06/02/1915
War Diary	Poperinghe	10/02/1915	13/02/1915
War Diary	Hondeghem	14/02/1915	27/02/1915
Heading	War Diary 14th Mobile Vet Section 3rd Cavalry Division For March 1915		
Heading	3rd Cavalry Division 14th Mobile Vety Lection Vol II		
War Diary	Hondeghem	01/03/1915	11/03/1915
War Diary	La Brearde	12/03/1915	12/03/1915
War Diary	Caudescure	13/03/1915	13/03/1915
War Diary	Hondeghem	14/03/1915	31/03/1915
Heading	Diary of 14 Mobile Vety Division 1-3-15 To 31-3-15		
Heading	War Diary of 14th Mobile Vet Section 3rd Cavalry Division April 1915		
Heading	3rd Cavalry Division 14th Mobile Vetinary Section Vol III 4-30.4.15		
War Diary	Hondeghem	04/04/1915	12/04/1915
War Diary	Renescure	13/04/1915	14/04/1915
War Diary	Cinqrues	14/04/1915	23/04/1915
War Diary	Hazebrouk	24/04/1915	25/04/1915
War Diary	Cinqrues	26/04/1915	30/04/1915
Heading	War Diary of 14 Mobile Veterinary Section 1st April 1915 To 30 April 1915		
Heading	War Diary of 3rd Cavalry Division For May-1915		
War Diary	Cinqrues	01/05/1915	28/05/1915
War Diary	Wardrecque	28/05/1915	31/05/1915

Heading	3rd Cavalry Division 14th Mobile Vety Sect Vol IV 1-31.5.15		
Heading	War Diary of 3rd Cavalry Division For June-1915		
Heading	3rd Cavalry Division 14th Mobile Vety Lection Vol V 4-29.6.15		
War Diary	Wardrecque	04/06/1915	29/06/1915
Heading	Diary 14th Mobile Vety Division June 1915		
Heading	War Diary of 14th Mobile Vet Section 3rd Cavalry Division July-1915		
Heading	3rd Cavalry Division 14th Mobile Vety Lection Vol VI		
War Diary	Wardrecque	01/07/1915	29/07/1915
Heading	War Diary of 14th Mobile Vet Section 3rd Cavalry Division August-1915		
Heading	3rd Cavalry Division 14th Mobile Vety Section Vol VII August 15		
War Diary	Wardrecque	01/08/1915	05/08/1915
War Diary	Westrehem	06/08/1915	11/08/1915
War Diary	Fauquembergues	13/08/1915	31/08/1915
Heading	War Diary of 14th Mobile Vet Section 3rd Cavalry Division September 1915		
Heading	3rd Cavalry Division 14th Mobile Vety. Section Vol VIII Sept 15		
War Diary	Fauquembergues	05/09/1915	21/09/1915
War Diary	Le Nieppe	22/09/1915	30/09/1915
Heading	War Diary of 14th Mobile Vet Section 3rd Cavalry Division October-1915		
Heading	3rd Cavalry Division 14th Mobile Vety. Section Vol IX Oct 15		
War Diary	Le Nieppe	03/10/1915	21/10/1915
War Diary	Fauquemberge	22/10/1915	25/10/1915
War Diary	Fauquemberge and Fruges	26/10/1915	31/10/1915
Heading	War Diary of 14th Mobile Vet Section 3rd Cavalry Division November December 1915		
Heading	14th Mobile Vety Sec Nov To Dec 1915 Vol XXI		
War Diary	Fauquemberge	02/11/1915	15/11/1915
War Diary	Verdure	16/11/1915	08/02/1916
War Diary	Bellevue	09/02/1916	14/03/1916
War Diary	Avesnes	15/03/1916	05/05/1916
War Diary	Hucqueliers	06/05/1916	12/05/1916
War Diary	Le Plouy	13/05/1916	15/05/1916
War Diary	L'Heure	16/05/1916	23/05/1916
War Diary	Hucqueliers	24/05/1916	26/06/1916
Heading	Bonnay	27/06/1916	04/07/1916
War Diary	Wanel	05/07/1916	08/07/1916
War Diary	Corbie	09/07/1916	01/08/1916
War Diary	Oissy	02/08/1916	02/08/1916
War Diary	Drugy	03/08/1916	04/08/1916
War Diary	Arcoules	05/08/1916	05/08/1916
War Diary	Hucqueliers	06/08/1916	10/09/1916
War Diary	Naintenay	11/09/1916	11/09/1916
War Diary	Brailly	12/09/1916	12/09/1916
War Diary	Yzeux	13/09/1916	15/09/1916
War Diary	La Neuville	16/09/1916	17/09/1916
War Diary	Between Daoyrs & Pt Noyelles	18/09/1916	24/09/1916
War Diary	Aix en Issart	25/09/1916	26/09/1916
War Diary	Fressin	27/09/1916	20/10/1916

War Diary	Planques	21/10/1916	01/02/1917
War Diary	Cucq	02/02/1917	05/04/1917
War Diary	Beauvainville	06/04/1917	09/04/1917
War Diary	Roads	10/04/1917	14/04/1917
War Diary	Roads 3 Kilos W of Arras	15/04/1917	16/04/1917
War Diary	Frohen Le Grand	17/04/1917	19/04/1917
War Diary	Tortefontaine	20/04/1917	13/05/1917
War Diary	Newbury	14/05/1917	15/05/1917
War Diary	Fouilloy	16/05/1917	17/05/1917
War Diary	Cerisy	18/05/1917	19/05/1917
War Diary	NE of Buire	20/05/1917	31/05/1917
War Diary	NE of Buire Sheet 62c Y22	01/06/1917	03/07/1917
War Diary	Suzanne	04/07/1917	08/07/1917
War Diary	Berles	09/07/1917	21/07/1917
War Diary	Rue de Guarbecques	24/07/1917	02/09/1917
War Diary	Bours	03/09/1917	10/10/1917
War Diary	Halametens of Lalonne en Lalonne Robelq Road	11/10/1917	24/10/1917
War Diary	Fieffes	25/10/1917	31/10/1917
War Diary	Franqueville	01/11/1917	20/11/1917
War Diary	Chuignolles	20/11/1917	23/11/1917
War Diary	La Houssoye	24/11/1917	02/12/1917
War Diary	Franvillers	03/12/1917	22/12/1917
War Diary	Barlette	23/12/1917	31/12/1917
War Diary	Fransu	01/01/1918	01/02/1918
War Diary	Trefcon	02/02/1918	13/03/1918
War Diary	Mereaucourt	14/03/1918	17/03/1918
War Diary	St Christ	18/03/1918	23/03/1918
War Diary	Carlepont	24/03/1918	27/03/1918
War Diary	Choisy au Back	28/03/1918	30/03/1918
War Diary	Sains En Amenois	31/03/1918	16/04/1918
War Diary	Bours	17/04/1918	30/04/1918
War Diary	Montigny	26/05/1918	31/05/1918
War Diary	Belloy Sur Somme	01/06/1918	14/06/1918
War Diary	Montigny	15/06/1918	22/06/1918
War Diary	St Owen	23/06/1918	30/06/1918
War Diary	Ouen	01/07/1918	16/07/1918
War Diary	St Ouen	01/07/1918	05/08/1918
War Diary	Bourdon	06/08/1918	06/08/1918
War Diary	Pont De Metz	07/08/1918	07/08/1918
War Diary	Boves	08/08/1918	09/08/1918
War Diary	Domart Sur La Luce	10/08/1918	12/08/1918
War Diary	Guyencourt	13/08/1918	15/08/1918
War Diary	St Ouen	16/08/1918	25/08/1918
War Diary	Le Boisle	26/08/1918	26/08/1918
War Diary	Conchy Sur Canche	27/08/1918	07/09/1918
War Diary	Boubers	08/09/1918	10/09/1918
War Diary	Willeman	11/09/1918	15/09/1918
War Diary	Rollencourt	16/09/1918	16/09/1918
War Diary	Field	17/09/1918	17/09/1918
War Diary	Willeman	18/09/1918	25/09/1918
War Diary	Orville	26/09/1918	26/09/1918
War Diary	Senlis	27/09/1918	27/09/1918
War Diary	Hem	28/09/1918	29/09/1918
War Diary	Vermand	30/09/1918	09/10/1918
War Diary	Bertry	10/10/1918	13/10/1918
War Diary	Bertincourt	14/10/1918	05/11/1918

War Diary	Sauchy Cauchy	06/11/1918	06/11/1918
War Diary	Planque	07/11/1918	07/11/1918
War Diary	Wahagnies	08/11/1918	09/11/1918
War Diary	Tourcoing	10/11/1918	15/11/1918
War Diary	Frasnes le Buissenal	16/11/1918	16/11/1918
War Diary	Moerbeke	17/11/1918	17/11/1918
War Diary	Castre	18/11/1918	20/11/1918
War Diary	Renival	21/11/1918	21/11/1918
War Diary	Maleves	22/11/1918	23/11/1918
War Diary	Jodinge-Souveraine	24/11/1918	14/12/1918
War Diary	Warnant	15/12/1918	15/12/1918
War Diary	Vien	16/12/1918	11/03/1919
War Diary	Nandrin	12/03/1919	31/03/1919
War Diary	Amay	01/04/1919	22/04/1919
War Diary	Amay	23/04/1919	23/04/1919
War Diary	Engis	24/04/1919	31/05/1919

WO 95/1149/3

1914-1919
3RD CAVALRY DIVISION

14TH MOBILE VETY SECTION

OCT 1914 - MAY 1919

WAR DIARY

OF

14th MOBILE VET. SECTION

3rd CAVALRY DIVISION

OCTOBER – DECEMBER 1914.

May 19.9

3C
QMD

121/4612

3rd Cavalry Division

14th Mobile Vety: Section

Vol I

Oct 1914

14th MOBILE VETERINARY SECTION

WAR DIARY
or
INTELLIGENCE SUMMARY.
(Erase heading not required.)

Army Form C. 2118.

Instructions regarding War Diaries and Intelligence Summaries are contained in F. S. Regs., Part II. and the Staff Manual, respectively. Title pages will be prepared in manuscript.

Hour, Date, Place	Summary of Events and Information	Remarks and references to Appendices
3rd Oct 1914 - 9.45 am WOOLWICH	Ordered by O.C. A.V.C Depot Woolwich to parade at 6.0 pm on 4-10-'14 to march "advance party" of 13th & 14th Mobile Veterinary Sections to Woolwich Railway Station to proceed to Portsmouth.	
4. Oct 1914. 9.0 am WOOLWICH	Proceeded to Portsmouth to draw equipment for the above two sections as laid down in "Mobilization Time Table" for a Mobile Veterinary Section Expeditionary Force.	
4. Oct 2.30 pm PORTSMOUTH	Arrived in Portsmouth. Proceeded to Ordnance Depot. Drew all equipment except "trace ends" and a few minor details which were not available then.	
9.0 pm	Proceeded by motor lorries (2) to Southampton	
4 Oct 11.30 pm S'HAMPTON	and arrived that night at Eleven Ave joined the there with the N.C.O & men of 13th & 14th Mobile Veterinary Sections.	

14th Mobile Vety Section

WAR DIARY
or
INTELLIGENCE SUMMARY.
(Erase heading not required.)

Army Form C. 2118.

Instructions regarding War Diaries and Intelligence Summaries are contained in F.S. Regs., Part II. and the Staff Manual respectively. Title pages will be prepared in manuscript.

Hour, Date, Place	Summary of Events and Information	Remarks and references to Appendices
5th October 1914. SOUTHAMPTON	Mobilization equipment drawn by me for 13th Mobile Vety Section, handed over to O.C. (W. Elam A.V.)	
" 10.0 a.m. "	15 remounts arrived from SALISBURY. 2 draught- and 13 riders. One draught horse was "Broken Winded." The others were sound. Fitting of harness and saddling was proceeded with, also rides for the men in order to get them accustomed to their new mounts.	
2nd Oct "	A light 4 wheeled cart was issued to my Section in lieu of "Cart pack." Proceeded to Docks with 14 Mobile Vety Section no nature by A.D.V.S. 3rd Division.	
6th October 5 p.m. "	Embarked for Havre.	

14th Mobile Veterinary Section

WAR DIARY
or
INTELLIGENCE SUMMARY.
(Erase heading not required.)

Army Form C. 2118.

Instructions regarding War Diaries and Intelligence Summaries are contained in F. S. Regs., Part II. and the Staff Manual respectively. Title pages will be prepared in manuscript.

Hour, Date, Place	Summary of Events and Information	Remarks and references to Appendices

Nominal Roll of 14th Mobile Vety Section as follows:-

Capt. E. Kearns AVC

No. 162	Sgt	T. Damon	AVC
335	Pte	T. Gurney	"
506	"	F. Burton	"
SR 24	"	A. Linford	"
SE 826	"	S. Smith Wykenin	"
SE 440	"	Cpl. Blank	"
SE 426	"	A. King	"
SE 429	"	T. Hutchins	"
SE 409	"	H. Pineham	"
SE 158	"	J.S. Dill	"
SE 326	"	St. Glover	"
22267	Driver	T. Oxley	AVC attached

1 Officer   12 NCO's & men

15 Horses.   1 Amb. (2 wheeler) limber

7 Sept 1914

Ot Sea

14 Mobile Veterinary Section

Army Form C. 2118.

WAR DIARY
or
INTELLIGENCE SUMMARY.
(Erase heading not required.)

Hour, Date, Place	Summary of Events and Information	Remarks and references to Appendices
8th October 1914 5 pm.	Disembarked at OSTEND. Proceeded to "Race Course" picketed for night	
9th October	The Broken Knee" mumps line received to Oculin was destroyed, so the journey from Docks to "Race Course" about 1½ miles was on mind for this reason the horses got low and sometimes the distraction.	
9th October 2.35 PM	Left OSTEND for BRUGES	
9th October 8.0 PM	Arrived at BRUGES	
10th October 8.0 PM	Arrived at OOSTCAMP took over his sick horses with "mumps" from "C Batty".	
11	Lt. OOSTCAMP put a good 2 miles beyond ZOORDERVORDE, reported to A.Q.2. 7 Cav B.S. I saw the Thro V.O's of the Brigade. He suggested that Colonel go to A.D.V.S. 3rd Cav Div and see if it were possible for me to establish a advance temporary hospital. so that they could have some fixed place to send their sick horses to.	

Form/C. 2118/10

WAR DIARY
or
INTELLIGENCE SUMMARY.

Army Form C. 2118.

Hour, Date, Place	Summary of Events and Information	Remarks and references to Appendices
March 1914	I reported the matter to the ADVS who was then at THOROUT. The ADVS gave me the following memo: "to go to Mobile Veterinary Section. Will you please proceed to BRUGES and from a Base Veterinary Hospital as far as possible with your mobile section. Sd. E.P. Barry Major ADVS 3.C.D."	
11th October 1914 BRUGES	I immediately proceeded to BRUGES & arrived at 10.30 p.m. I met Lt. Col. No 12 Mobile Vety Section there, and he had already established a temporary hospital for the 7th Infantry Division. There were some sick horses belonging to the 62nd Cav. Bde and "K" Battery which Lt. Col. No 12 Mobile Vety Section was looking after. These horses were chiefly suffering from "Strangles"	

14th Mobile Vety Section

WAR DIARY
or
INTELLIGENCE SUMMARY.
(Erase heading not required.)

Army Form C. 2118.

Instructions regarding War Diaries and Intelligence Summaries are contained in F. S. Regs., Part II. and the Staff Manual respectively. Title pages will be prepared in manuscript.

Hour, Date, Place		Summary of Events and Information	Remarks and references to Appendices
11th Oct 1914	BRUGES	However before that time to adopted my section and wrote in with 12 Mobile V. Section. Received a Telegram from A.D.V.S. 3rd Cav Div. who was then at ROULERS "to evacuate my section from BRUGES immediately and proceed by road to DUNKIRQUE. The O.C. 12th Section was away at the time, so I left a copy of my Telegram with his senior sergeant for his information when he returned.	
	2.30 pm	I marched out of BRUGES en route for DUNKIRQUE	
12th October 1914 CASTRELLES	4.0 PM	Arrived at CASTRELLES and picketted out for the night	
13th Oct FOURES 8.30 P.M		Proceeded to FOURES. Refugees were very close away to Ostrejero on the road from OSTEND	
14. Oct DUNKIRQUE 7.30 PM		Arrived at DUNKIRQUE and reported to Base Commandant. who ordered me to hand over my horses and wagon to O.C. 12th Mobile Vety Section (which Section had arrived from BRUGES via OSTEND by Train) and then to embark on the	

WAR DIARY
or
INTELLIGENCE SUMMARY.

Army Form C. 2118.

Hour, Date, Place	Summary of Events and Information	Remarks and references to Appendices
	S.S. DIEPPE with my section and proceed to BOULOGNE. Am and receive all sick horses sent by train	
14th Oct 1914 9.30 pm	Entrained with 12 NCOs & men, and equipment on S.S. Dieppe	
15th Oct 1914 4.30 pm	Arrived at BOULOGNE. The R.T.O. reported to me that there were some sick horses from the 3rd Cavalry Division in trucks at the Railway Station, which I immediately attended to and brought to my temporary camp near the Station. Every day there were sick horses coming to BOULOGNE from the 3rd Cavalry Division and other formations. I returned to 2 or 3 sick horses during my stay at BOULOGNE, 16 of which died or — the train or died soon after arrival, or discharged as incurable.	

WAR DIARY
or
INTELLIGENCE SUMMARY.
(Erase heading not required.)

Army Form C. 2118.

Hour, Date, Place	Summary of Events and Information	Remarks and references to Appendices
20th Oct 1914	By an N.C.O. and 30 men I sent by train to HAVRE Vety. Hospital 197 sick horses, one man per horse. It however were supplied with forage for the journey. I had great difficulty in dealing with this large number of sick horses, as I only had my small Vety Section erected by 20 civilians. However my men were very willing, and worked well under The circs. — The D.D.V.S. G.H.Q ordered me to evacuate — These sick arrived at HAVRE, and then proceed to Railway with my Section.	197
21st Oct. BOULOGNE	Proceeded to PONT DE BRIQUES and took over my section horses & wagon from 12 Section Amb. Entrained for Railway 3rd Coun Div.	
22nd Oct "	Departed from BOULOGNE 10.30 p.m.	
23rd Oct CASTRE	Arrived CASTRE, and proceeded by road to LOCRE	

4 Mobile Veterinary Section

WAR DIARY
or
INTELLIGENCE SUMMARY.
(Erase heading not required.)

Army Form C. 2118.

Instructions regarding War Diaries and Intelligence Summaries are contained in F.S. Regs., Part II. and the Staff Manual respectively. Title pages will be prepared in manuscript.

Hour, Date, Place		Summary of Events and Information	Remarks and references to Appendices
22nd Oct 1914	YPRES	Arrived YPRES, and reported my arrival to A.D.V.S. 3rd Cav. Div. at Zonne ZEELEBEKE	
25th Oct	ZEELEBEKE	Billeted at ZEELEBEKE	
26th Oct	"	42 Sick horses collected & sent by rail from YPRES to ABBEVILLE Vety. Hospital	42
29th October	"	41 Sick horses entrained at YPRES & sent to ABBEVILLE	41
30th October	"	12 " " " " "	12
31st October	"	5 " " " " "	5
2nd November 1914		Proceeded from ZEELEBEKE to a farm halfway between YPRES & VLAMERTINGHE & established a Horse Depot for 3rd Cav Division in conjunction with my Veterinary duties, by order of A.A. & Q.M.G. 3rd Cav Div. Through my A.D.V.S. The reason was as the particular period every available cavalry soldier was needed in the Trenches. I took over 127 Remounts and the various units billeted round YPRES to like them over	Adverse Expense on no Mobile Veterinarian

A.E. [signature] 2nd
4 [Nov] 1914

14 Mobile Veterinary Section

WAR DIARY or INTELLIGENCE SUMMARY.
(Erase heading not required.)

Army Form C. 2118.

Instructions regarding War Diaries and Intelligence Summaries are contained in F. S. Regs., Part II. and the Staff Manual respectively. Title pages will be prepared in manuscript.

Hour, Date, Place	Summary of Events and Information	Remarks and references to Appendices
4th Nov 1914 VLAMERTINGHE - YPRES	22 sick horses sent from POPERINGHE to ABBEVILLE	22
5th Nov 1914	114 sick and inefficient animals hospitalled from POPERINGHE to ABBEVILLE	114
	3 horses destroyed. (1 septic pneumonia, 2 punctured wounds)	
	1 horse died of a wound (shrapnel wound)	
9th Nov 1914 YPRES-VLAMERTINGHE	104 sick horses sent from BAILLEUL to ABBEVILLE	104
	Up to this date all animals (127) were received to unit in the 3rd Cav. Bdiv. according to orders from O.M.G. French A.D.V.S.	
11th Nov 1914 " "	46 sick horses sent from POPERINGHE to ABBEVILLE	46
15th Nov 1914 " "	117 sick " "	117
16th Nov 1914 " "	29 sick " "	29
17th Nov 1914 " "	171 Remounts received in 3rd Corps Depot under my charge. In re-issue to units under A.A. & Q.M.G.'s arrangements.	
19th Nov 1914 " "	65 sick horses sent from POPERINGHE to ABBEVILLE	65

WAR DIARY
or
INTELLIGENCE SUMMARY.
(Erase heading not required.)

Army Form C. 2118.

Instructions regarding War Diaries and Intelligence Summaries are contained in F. S. Regs., Part II. and the Staff Manual respectively. Title pages will be prepared in manuscript.

Hour, Date, Place	Summary of Events and Information	Remarks and references to Appendices
20th Nov '14 YPRES. VLAM. INGHE	14 Sick horses sent from POPERINGHE to ABBEVILLE. All remounts (171) issued to units as directed by A.A. & Q.M.G. 2nd Cav. Div.	14
21st Nov '14 " STRAZEELE	13 Sick horses sent from POPERINGHE to ABBEVILLE. Proceeded with the Section to STRAZEELE. Billeted there for night.	13
22nd Nov '14 HAZEBROUCK	Arrived at HAZEBROUCK reported to A.D.V.S. 2 Cav Div & 5 men joined the Section. The A.D.V.S. ordered me to proceed to H.Q. 2nd 7 Div. 2 Bde at HONDEGHEM	
23rd " " HONDEGHEM	4 men A.V.C. joined Section for duty.	
29th " " "	16 Sick horses sent from HAZEBROUCK to ABBEVILLE.	16
		Edward Smith Lt. in Charge Mob. Section

Form/C. 2118/10

4 Mobile Veterinary Section

WAR DIARY
or
INTELLIGENCE SUMMARY.
(Erase heading not required.)

Army Form C. 2118.

Instructions regarding War Diaries and Intelligence Summaries are contained in F. S. Regs., Part II. and the Staff Manual respectively. Title pages will be prepared in manuscript.

Hour, Date, Place	Summary of Events and Information	Remarks and references to Appendices
1st December 1914 HAZEBROUCK	16 sick horses sent from HAZEBROUCK to ABBEVILLE	16
8th "	40	40
10th "	61	61
11th "	57	57
14th "	32	32
19th "	16 " BOULOGNE	16
23rd "	8 " NEUFCHATEL	8
26th "	12 " "	12
30th "	6 " "	6

Ephraim Left?
O.C. 4 Mobile Vety Section

WAR DIARY

OF

14TH MOBILE VET SECTION

3RD CAVALRY DIVISION

JAN & FEB – 1915

14 Mobile Veterinary Section

Army Form C. 2118.

WAR DIARY
or
INTELLIGENCE SUMMARY.
(Erase heading not required.)

Instructions regarding War Diaries and Intelligence Summaries are contained in F. S. Regs., Part II. and the Staff Manual respectively. Title pages will be prepared in manuscript.

Hour, Date, Place	Summary of Events and Information	Remarks and references to Appendices
4th Jany 1915. HONDGHEM	21 sick horses sent from HAZEBROUCK to NEUFCHATEL	21
	1 remount	" for Remt. Depot
9th Jany 1915	13 sick horses " " " NEUFCHATEL	13
	1 Remount " " " for Remt Depot	
29th Jany 1915	14 sick horses " " " NEUFCHATEL	14
		E. Oram Capt
		OC 14 M.V. Section

Form/C. 2118/10

14 Mobile Veterinary Section

WAR DIARY
or
INTELLIGENCE SUMMARY.

Army Form C. 2118.

Hour, Date, Place	Summary of Events and Information	Remarks and references to Appendices
1st Feb 1915 HONDEGHEM	8 sick horses sent from HAZEBROUK to NEUFCHATEL	8
2nd Feb "	1 sick " (mange) "	1
"	This horse belonged to 15.84 R.H.A.	
4?	Paid G.S. Swingle 10½ francs for keep of abandoned horse unable to travel belonging to 10th R. Hussars	
	Paid M Pothin 10½ francs for keep of abandoned horse belonging to X R Hussars	
	Paid Julian Borkin 10½ francs for abandoned horse unable to travel belonging to Bear Yeomanry	
	Paid Madame Delfosse 66 francs for keep of a sick horse unable to travel belonging to 27th Division	
	Paid M Loots 37 francs for keep of abandoned horse unable to travel belonging to 27th Division	
6th Feb	Exchanged a horse of the 3rd B.G.S which here had borrow its work in HAZEBROUK sent report sent to V.O i/c 3rd B.G.S	

14 Mobile Veterinary Section

WAR DIARY
or
INTELLIGENCE SUMMARY.
(Erase heading not required.)

Army Form C. 2118.

Instructions regarding War Diaries and Intelligence Summaries are contained in F.S. Regs, Part II. and the Staff Manual respectively. Title pages will be prepared in manuscript.

Hour, Date, Place	Summary of Events and Information	Remarks and references to Appendices
10th Feb 1915 POPERINGHE	Arrived with a detachment of 14 Section for duty with 3rd Cav Div who were in the trenches. Reported to A.A. & Q.M.G. also entrained the three transport wagons 15.? 7? -F? Cav B as.	
11th Feb "	Established nr home H.Q. Before suffering severely from laminitis, unable to walk. Sent upon cart to V.O. I/c	
13. Feb "	Went to YPRES & removed some sick horses	
14. Feb "	Jack horse ant from POPERINGHE to NEUFCHATEL	?
15. " " HONDEGHEM	Left POPERINGHE arrived back to HONDEGHEM. Post mortem examination on a horse 4th 61st Co A.S.C. – In the absence of A.V.C. who was on leave, case reported to V.O. I/c on his return.	
16. ? "	Jack horses sent from STEENBECQUE to NEUFCHATEL. Discharged one horse of the 7th Divl F.? Amb. Still suffering from "laminitis". – by order of A.D.V.S.	?
16.? Feb	Sells Lynny Hutchens & Wilkins transferred to No 10 Vety. Hospital BASE	

14 Mobile Vety Sectn

WAR DIARY
or
INTELLIGENCE SUMMARY.
(Erase heading not required.)

Army Form C. 2118.

Hour, Date, Place	Summary of Events and Information	Remarks and references to Appendices
23rd July 1915 HONDEGHEM	40 Sick horses sent from STEENBECQUE to NEUFCHATEL	40
26th July "	Cpl T Girvan ASC transferred to No.10 Vety Hospital Base.	
27th " "	Sick horses despatched from HAZEBROUCK to NEUFCHATEL 9	9
	1 mangy " " " " "	
	16 sick " " " " "	16
		Etienne Hipp?
		OC 14 Mobile Vety Sectn

WAR DIARY

of

14th MOBILE VET SECTION.

3rd CAVALRY DIVISION

FOR

MARCH 1915

3C/131/4607

AUD

3rd Cavalry Division

14th Mobile Vety: Section.

Vol II

14 MOBILE VETERINARY SECTION.

Army Form C. 2118.

WAR DIARY
or
INTELLIGENCE SUMMARY.
(Erase heading not required.)

Instructions regarding War Diaries and Intelligence Summaries are contained in F.S. Regs., Part II. and the Staff Manual respectively. Title pages will be prepared in manuscript.

4617

Hour, Date, Place	Summary of Events and Information	Remarks and references to Appendices
1st March 19/15 HONDEGHEM	10 sick horses evacuated to NEUFCHATEL 2 remounts SE 326 Chound-Smith A.H. UPPERTON ave transferred to No 10 Vety Hospital in order of DDVS Cav Corps.	10
2.3.15	T35420 Dnr S Torvo ARC joined 14. M.V.S. 5pm 35466 " A. GREE ARC " " " Base Horse Transport Depot. as Linkeepers	GREE
3.3.15	2687 Pte S.F. Cook ARC joined for duty 14 M.V.S. Two abandoned horses collected near HAZEBROUCK belonging to R.H.A. & S.L. Lancers. The horse belonging to S.L. Lancers was destroyed as incurable. Cause gunshot. A destruct mare 14. M.V.S ran	
4.3.15	away with Briefields bunch off 14 M.V.S. The mare broke its neck. The interpreter went to hospital injured. I investigated the matter came to the conclusion that this was purely accidental	

14. MOBILE VET'Y SECTION

WAR DIARY
or
INTELLIGENCE SUMMARY.
(Erase heading not required.)

Army Form C. 2118.

Hour, Date, Place			Summary of Events and Information	Remarks and references to Appendices
6.	8.15	HONDEGHEM	6 Sick horses dispatched to NEUFCHATEL	8
10.	3.15	"	19 " " " "	19
			1 mare in foal " " "	
			1 remount " " "	
11.	3.15	"	Proceeded to LA BREARDE with section for night- out for night-	
12.	3.15	LA BREARDE	11 sick horses dispatched to NEUFCHATEL	11
			Proceeded to CAUDESCURE with Section	
13.	3.15	CAUDESCURE	Reported to H.Qrs. 7 Cav. Bde my arrival	
			Left one man A.V.C. with 2 sick horses 1st Life Guards	
			near CAUDESCURE	
			Returned to original billet	
14.	3.15	HONDEGHEM	arrived at HONDEGHEM with Section	
15.	3.15	"	26 Sick horses dispatched to NEUFCHATEL	26
16.	3.15	"	Sick horse abandoned by Canadian Divsni cellulse	
			near BLAZE BROUK.	
			Ch. mare abandoned by 1st Brid 2 Divi Ammn Col collected	
			near CASSEL.	

14 MOBILE VETY SECTION

Army Form C. 2118.

WAR DIARY
or
INTELLIGENCE SUMMARY.
(Erase heading not required.)

Instructions regarding War Diaries and Intelligence Summaries are contained in F.S. Regs., Part II. and the Staff Manual respectively. Title pages will be prepared in manuscript.

Hour, Date, Place	Summary of Events and Information	Remarks and references to Appendices
15.3.15 HONDEGHEM	Stray mule belonging to 1st Midland Div. collected nr CASSEL	
16.3.15 "	8 sick horses dispatched to NEUFCHATEL	8
19.3.15 "	Went to CAUDESCURE to visit 2 sick horses 1st L.GA	
20.3.15 "	Above 2 horses 1 L.GB brought to M.V.S. SE 3359 PG K. FLETCHER. Avc June 14 M.V.S. SE 644 PG A. WHEATLAND Avc admitted to Hospital. Kick from a horse.	
21.3.15 "		
22.3.15 "	13 sick horses & 1 mule dispatched to NEUFCHATEL. Took over charge of Hqrs 3 Car Div 3rd field Squadron 3rd Signal Squadron & & Co ASC from Lt COOPER AVC transferred to Base.	13 (1)
24.3.15	8 sick horses dispatched to NEUFCHATEL. Driver Oxley AVC (22267) transferred to Hospital	8

Forms/C. 2118/10

14. MOBILE VETY SECTION

WAR DIARY
or
INTELLIGENCE SUMMARY.
(Erase heading not required.)

Army Form C. 2118.

Hour, Date, Place	Summary of Events and Information	Remarks and references to Appendices
25.3.15 HONDEGHEM	S.E. 37 Stound-Smith & WATT. AVC joined 14 MVS for duty.	
26.3.15 "	S.S. Cpl W GOURLAY AVC transferred to No 1 Vety Hospital auth. DDVS Cav Corps.	
27.3.15 "	8 sick horses inspected 5 NEUFCHATEL. 5.	
31.3.15 "	1 mare infoal, 1 remount - vice 5 dispatched to No 10 Veterinary Hospital NEUFCHATEL	

E Neame Capt
O.C.
14 Mobile Veterinary Section.

CONFIDENTIAL

DIARY of
14 Mobile Vety. Section
1-3-15 to 31-3-15

WAR DIARY

OF

14th MOBILE VET. SECTION

3rd CAVALRY DIVISION

APRIL 1915

121/5255

3rd Cavalry Division

14th Mobile Veterinary Section.

Vol III — 4 — 30.4.15

WAR DIARY
or
INTELLIGENCE SUMMARY.
(Erase heading not required.)

Army Form C. 2118.

Hour, Date, Place	Summary of Events and Information	Remarks and references to Appendices
April 4th HONDEGHEM	Sick horse belonging to Divisional Train destroyed at 4 M.V.S. Cause: Open hock joint. Death report sent to V.O. i/c Div. yo.	
April 5 HONDEGHEM	10 sick horses dispatched to No 10 Vety Hospital	10
April 7 "	8 " " " " " " "	8
April 12 "	10 " " " " " " "	10
RENESCURE	Proceeded to RENESCURE and section picketed out for night. Four animals evacuated for section	
April 13th	Visited HONDEGHEM to enquire if any hand horses had been billeted there, as it was reported that a Battery had passed through, in the billets some cases of "Mange" had been reported. The section on "marching order" was inspected by the D.D.V.S. 2nd Corps	
April 14th RENESCURE	Proceeded to CINQ RUES, near HAZEBROUCK to view of probable repair of horse B of billets there	
CINQ RUES		
April 15 CINQ RUES	8 sick horses dispatched to No 10 Vety Hospital	8

Army Form C. 2118.

WAR DIARY
or
INTELLIGENCE SUMMARY.
(Erase heading not required.)

Instructions regarding War Diaries and Intelligence Summaries are contained in F.S. Regs., Part II. and the Staff Manual respectively. Title pages will be prepared in manuscript.

Hour, Date, Place	Summary of Events and Information	Remarks and references to Appendices
April 17th BINQUES	14 Sick horses & 1 mule on foot despatched to No 10 Vety Hosp. sta NEUFCHATEL	14
April 19th CAMBRES	9 sick horses despatched to NEUFCHATEL	9
April 21st	8 " " " "	8
April 22nd	Proceeded with part of my section to ST JAN CAPPEL & collected 9 sick horses for evacuation from 158th RHA	
April 23rd	Returned to REINQUES	
April 24th HAZEBROUK	27 sick horses despatched to NEUFCHATEL. Took over charge of 46 remounts from ADVR Horse.	27
April 25th "	Inspected no units were unable to draw them	
" "	Handed over 46 remounts to Remount Officer and parks	
April 26th CAMBRES	10 men sent from my section to Lille remount to convey railhead	10
April 27th "	10 sick horses despatched to NEUFCHATEL	11
April 28th "	8 " " "	8
April 29th "	17 " " "	17
April 30th "	4 " " "	4

Adrienne Sapt [signature]
OC 14. "Mobile Vety Section"

Forms/C. 2118/10

Confidential

War Diary

of

14 Mobile Veterinary Section

October 1915 & 30 April 1915

WAR DIARY

OF

1/4th MOBILE VET. SECTION.

3RD CAVALRY DIVISION

FOR

MAY - 1915

WAR DIARY
or
INTELLIGENCE SUMMARY.

(Erase heading not required.)

Army Form C. 2118.

May 1915

(23)

Hour, Date, Place	Summary of Events and Information	Remarks and references to Appendices
1st May Cing Rues	Proceeded to FORGES nr POPERINGHE with 5 men and fetched 10 sick horses from 7th Cavalry Brigade. Returned to CINQ RUES	
3rd May CINQ RUES	Same rate. Dispatched 14 sick horses to NEUFCHATEL viz I L Gds 6; II L Gds 1; LEI YEO 4; 15 Hrs 2; 3rd Cav Div Sqn 1; total 14.	14
4th May 1915 CINQ RUES	Dispatched 6 French horses to NEUFCHATEL viz. 5th F Sqd RE 2; LEI YEO. 2; II L Gds 1; 3rd Cav Sqd RE 1.	6
5th May 1915	Staff Sgt Fox Rogers are, 2 Cpls J H Walls, + W Leake transferred to Base for duty.	
6th May 1915 "	Dispatched 6 sick horses to NEUFCHATEL viz 15 Hrs 4; 3rd F Sqd RE 2. R S M W Clifford & Rough attendant to Hospital enfiend from (Veterinary)	6
7th May 1915 "	14 horses cast by R A V C Cav Corps. Entrained 16 15 Hussars, unloaded 16 Base. 2 horses transferred to Remount Depot THIENNES from 15 Hussars, for Br Bde Cav Corps	

WAR DIARY or INTELLIGENCE SUMMARY

Army Form C. 2118.

May 1915

(24)

Hour, Date, Place	Summary of Events and Information	Remarks and references to Appendices
8th May 1915 VINA RUES	6 sick horses + one mare in foal evacuated to NEUF-CHATEL: N3, 1S Sqd 3; 3 Can Bn HQ 2; 81 Co RSC 1; 7 CBH 1.	7
10th " "	18 sick horses evacuated to NEUFCHATEL: N3, II Sqd 11; II L Gd 3; LEI Y EO. 4.	18
11th " "	5 sick horses evacuated to NEUFCHATEL: N3, G/S Sqd Can Corps. 3; II L Gd 2.	5
14th " "	5 sick horses evacuated to NEUFCHATEL: N3, LEI Y EO. 3; 3 Can Div HQ 1. 3F.S Sqd. RE 1.	5
15th " "	29 surplus H.D. horses emerged from 13th Hussars and one H.D horse from 9 Can B. 2 HQs and handed over to O.C. Remount Depot THIENNES by order of B.O.V.S. Can Corps for 2.A O.R Can Corps.	
18th " "	Evacuated 6 sick horses + 1 sick mule to NEUFCHATEL N3, II Sqd 2; 3 Can Div HAR 1; 81 Co RSC 2; 14 MVS 1 ORE; Vol Corps mule 1	7

Form C. 2118/10

WAR DIARY or INTELLIGENCE SUMMARY

Army Form C. 2118.

(25) (May 1915)

Hour, Date, Place	Summary of Events and Information	Remarks and references to Appendices
19.? May 1915 LINQ RUES	4675 Pd. L.Cp. Lambert of 2.B.4?. transferred to No 9 M.V.S.	
22nd May 1915 "	6 horses evacuated to NEUFCHATEL, viz, LEI.YEO. 2; 2? ?.7d Amb. 1; 5 Lancs Fus. 1.	6
24. ? "	8 sick horses evacuated to NEUFCHATEL, viz, L. Bde. RHA 5; LEI. YEO. 2; ? Cav. B4 HQ 1.	
25.? "	11 sick horses evacuated to NEUFCHATEL, viz. I.I.96 8; II.L.9? 3.	8
27.? "	Reinforcement 1 Rider for 14. M.V.S. 12 sick horses evacuated to NEUFCHATEL, viz, LEI.YEO. 9; II.96 1; 7? L.B HQ 1; 3F.Sq.RE 1.	12
28.? "	14 sick horses evacuated to NEUFCHATEL, viz, LEI.YEO. 9; II.L.9? 3; 3rd F.Sq.RE 2.	14
WARDRECQUE	Proceeded from LINQ RUES to WARDRECQUE via STEENBECQUE. Arrived with Section at WARDRECQUE.	
31st May 1915 "	Evacuated one Suspected Stein case to NEUFCHATEL.	1

121/5513

3rd Cavalry Division

14th Mobile Vety. Sect.

Vol IV 1 — 31. 5. 15.

War Diary

of

14th Mobile Vet. Section

3rd Cavalry Division

for

June - 1915.

3rd Cavalry Division

121/5935

14 tk hostile Vtg: lecker

Vol V 4 — 29.6.15.

AVD

Army Form C. 2118.

26

WAR DIARY
or
INTELLIGENCE SUMMARY.

June 1915

(Erase heading not required.)

Instructions regarding War Diaries and Intelligence Summaries are contained in F.S. Regs., Part II. and the Staff Manual respectively. Title pages will be prepared in manuscript.

Hour, Date, Place	Summary of Events and Information	Remarks and references to Appendices
WARDRECQUE 4.6.15	Collected a sick horse belonging to 7?? Can Bde afpr. from VLAMERTINGHE	
" 7.6.15	Dispatched 4 sick horses from STEEN BECQUE to NEUFCHATEL	4
" 10.6.15	11 Remount cases cast by 8 ADR Car Corps collected from units evacuated from OSTEN BECQUE to No 10 Vety Hospital	
" 11.6.15	Abandoned horse of 12?? Div evacuated at RENESCURE. This horse was suffering from Pleurisy and died soon after. June 21st.	
" 10.6.15	11 horses transferred to THIENNES Remount Field Section for SADR Car. Corps.	
" 10.6.15	8 sick horses evacuated to No.10 Vety Hospital Base. Also 2 mares in foal.	8
" 16.6.15	9 sick horses & one mare and foal dispatched to No.10 Vety Hospital Base	9
" 22.6.15	7 sick horses evacuated to Base	7

Army Form C. 2118.

WAR DIARY
or
INTELLIGENCE SUMMARY.   June, 1915
(Erase heading not required.)

Instructions regarding War Diaries and Intelligence Summaries are contained in F. S. Regs., Part II. and the Staff Manual respectively. Title pages will be prepared in manuscript.

Hour, Date, Place	Summary of Events and Information	Remarks and references to Appendices
WARDRECQUE 29.6.15.	3 horses cast in SADR. C.C. evacuated from STEENBECQUE to Base.	
	4 sick horses evacuated to No. 0 Vety Hospital	4
	30.6.'15	
		Edmund Leigh
		ac. 14 Mobile Vety. Section

Forms/C. 2118/10

Diary
of
14th Mobile Vety
Section

June 1915

War Diary

of

14th Mobile Vet Section

3rd Cavalry Division

July – 1915.

137/62/14

avo

3rd Cavalry Division

the bastille vety: section
14

Vol VII

1 - 2 9 - - 1 -

WAR DIARY
or
INTELLIGENCE SUMMARY.

(28)

Army Form C. 2118

Hour, Date, Place	Summary of Events and Information	Remarks and references to Appendices
1st July WARDRECQUES	8 sick horses evacuated to No 10 Vety Hospital from STEENBECQUE	8
2nd "	2 horses suffering from "lice" returned to 1st Life Guards as cured.	
"	2 horses cast by RAVC have horses evacuated to Base	
3rd "	8 sick horses evacuated to No 10 Vety Hospital	8
4th "	8 sick horses " " " " "	8
"	1 Officer's charger " to BOULOGNE Remt Depot by mer of 5th A.V.D. War Corps.	
5th "	2 horses cast by RAVC have horses evacuated	
13th "	6 sick horses evacuated to No 10 Vety Hospital	6
"	1 mule cast by RAVC have horses evacuated to BOULOGNE	
14th "	10 sick horses evacuated to No 10 Vety Hospital	10
"	Lpl. Parker W.M.H.S. transferred to X X 2 M.V.S. for duty.	
15th "	5333 Pte. Newman 600? transferred to Emr Reinforcements, ROUEN	

WAR DIARY
INTELLIGENCE SUMMARY.
(Erase heading not required.)

Army Form C. 2118

(29)

14th MOBILE VETERINARY SECTION
Date July

Hour, Date, Place	Summary of Events and Information	Remarks and references to Appendices
19 July 15 WARDRECQUES	SE37 SS Cpl Watt transferred to No 13 Vety Hospital 237 L/Cpl A Philcox " " No 5 " SE4939 L/S EW Allen arrived at 14 M.V.S. for duty. SE3020 Pte GA Ball admitted to hospital sick to R Hosp	
21 July 15	Four sick horses admitted by infantry collected	
23rd "	6354 Pte M Lynch 70 gd transferred to country	
"	Reinforcements ROUEN	
26 "	8 sick horses transferred to No 10 Vety Hospital	8
"	4 " " attended by infantry collected awaiting rites left mid farmers	
27 "	5 LD horses handed over to Lt D.G.D by order of ADVS Bear Depôt	
"	2 sick horses & one mule collected from WISNES attended by infantry	
28 "	11 sick horses transferred to No 10 Vety Hospital	11

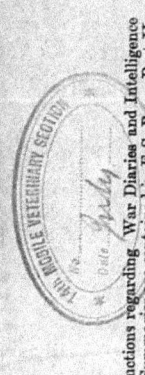

Lalonne Capt
O.C. 14 M.V.S. 31 July 1915

War Diary

of

14th Mobile Vet. Section

3rd Cavalry Division

August - 1915.

121/581

3rd Cavalry Division

14th Mobile Vety Section.

Part VII

August 15.

WAR DIARY
or
INTELLIGENCE SUMMARY.

Army Form C. 2118

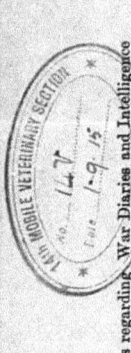

Hour, Date, Place	Summary of Events and Information	Remarks and references to Appendices
1st August 1915 WARDRECQUE	Collected two abandoned Gov. horses belonging to 20" Div. one at LYNDE + one at RENESCURE	
2nd August 1915	7 Sick horses evacuated to N°. 10 Vety Hospital	7.
6 August - WESTREHEM.	Proceeded with Section to WESTREHEM.	
	Abandoned sick horse collected. 17 Div. one horse at WAVRANS. 20th Div. one horse at REMILLY WIRQUIN. Two horses belonging to 93rd Bde RFA at AVROULT. Mules 92nd Bde. RFA at MERICK ST LEVIN. Also another here	
	Left at	
9th Aug NESTREHEM.	17 Sick horses evacuated to N°. 10 Vety Hospital	17.
10 Aug "	Stay continued by Capt Jones A.V.C. who with look took over the M. Mobile Vet Section from Capt Hearne AVC	
11 Aug "	Proceeded with Section to FAUQUEMBERGUES arriving at 1.30 A.M. To be attached independent all division horse.	
13 Aug - FAUQUEMBERGUES	Collected one abandoned horse of IV Decan Horse from WANDONNE and one mule and one horse g N Bty from RADINGHEM. Afternoon went to ARQUES & WIZERNES adjust sending horses to the there hospitals	By Team Sgt A.V.C. to N. Mobile Vet Sect.

14th Mobile Veterinary Sect.

WAR DIARY
INTELLIGENCE SUMMARY
(Erase heading not required.)

Army Form C. 2118

14th Mobile Veterinary Section
No. 14 V
Date 3.1-8.15

Hour, Date, Place	Summary of Events and Information	Remarks and references to Appendices
16 August FAUQUEMBERGUES	Eight sick horses and one mule evacuated from LUMBRES Rly to Vety Hospital.	9
17 August	Also Sergt. Fr. R. DADD, M. Charge of late Lieut PEAKE. 15th Mounted depot BOULOGNE for shipment to England.	1
22 August	Inspected 4th Bde Ammunition Col RHA at Campagne Vieille and R. Schier RAMC at RADINGHEM	
23 August to 31 August	Collected one sick horse of 126" Bde RFA from BONNIQUES to two to Vety Hospt. 25 Sick Horses Evacuated.	1 25
	Nothing of note to report outside usual routine work.	

R.O. Jann
Capt AVC
OC 14 Mobile Vety Sect.

War Diary

of

14th Mobile Vet Section

3rd Cavalry Division

September - 1915

121/6923

3rd Cavalry Division

14 br bertild vetp: leedon

Vol VIII

Sept. 15

14 Mobile Veterinary Section.
7 Cav Bde.

WAR DIARY
or
INTELLIGENCE SUMMARY.
(Erase heading not required.)   September

Army Form C. 2118.

Hour, Date, Place	Summary of Events and Information	Remarks and references to Appendices
3rd September FAUQUEMBERGUES	Evacuated 19 Sick horses from LUMBRES to No 10 Vety Hospital, and one horse cast by the DADR	19 / 1
8 September "	Collected at MESNIL near DOHEM one horse cast by 75 Bde R.F.A Guards Division	1
13 September "	Evacuated 9 horses cast by the DADR and 20 Sick horses from LUMBRES to No 10 Veterinary Hospital.	9 / 20
14 September "	Clinics at section. Nine lame horses of 46 D.A.C were made to trampeal on the street. Took over temporary charge of 20 H.VS and g/adrs in addition to ordinary routine work.	3
16 September		
17 + 18 September "		
19 September "	Evacuated from LUMBRES the sick horses and standing by for orders regarding a move.	10
20 September - 9 P.M.	Received orders to move at 8 A.M next morning	
21 September	Marched at 9.40 A.M. and arrived at LE NIEPPE at 4 P.M.	
22 September LE NIEPPE	Two troopers of units	
25 September "	Capt Richardson received orders to report 15 ADVS 3 Cav Divn and proceeded forthwith, leaving two VO's and Brigade	

14th Mobile Vety Section
7' Cav Bde.

WAR DIARY
or
INTELLIGENCE SUMMARY.

Army Form C. 2118.

(33)

September

14th MOBILE VETERINARY Date 30.9.15

Hour, Date, Place	Summary of Events and Information	Remarks and references to Appendices
26th September LE NIEPPE	Evacuated 10 sick horses from ARQUES to No 10 Veterinary Hospital.	10
27 September -	Inspected horses B.K. Btty and 'A' & 'B' Echelon Cols	
28 September -	Inspected 7 Cav Bde Field Ambulance horses.	
29 & 30 -	Inspection duty. Closed Diary for the month.	

P. A. Jamm
Cap' AVC
OC 14th Mobile Veterinary Section.
7 Cav Bde.

WAR DIARY

OF

14th MOBILE VET. SECTION

3rd CAVALRY DIVISION

OCTOBER - 1915

21/7376

a/s

3ʳᵈ Cavalry Division

14th Reptile Vol: Sector

Vt x

Oct 15

11th Mobile Veterinary Section

WAR DIARY
or
INTELLIGENCE SUMMARY.   October   No 34

Army Form C. 2118.

Hour, Date, Place	Summary of Events and Information	Remarks and references to Appendices
3rd October 1915 LE NIEPPE	Proceeded to St SYLVESTRE CAPPEL and inspected the sick horse. Also to SERCUS to inspect the sick horse.	
4 October "	Collected one sick horse left by the 2nd Canadian Divl: train at ST. SYLVESTRE. Also collected three horses of 4.103rd Bde R.F.A. left at SERCUS. Four had been left but one had died of Pneumonia before a.m. 9.15 from pneumonia. Evacuated these horses together with seven more from CAESTRE to No 10 Veterinary Hospital.	4 Horses Collected 1 11 Evacuated
6 October "	Visited the Horses of 2nd Army Head Quarters at CASSEL. Proceeded to the farm of M. DEQUIDT near STAPLE to collect one horse, and found the horse had already been collected.	
7th to 10 October "	Standing by, and normal routine work shoeing &c	
11 October "	Evacuated eight sick horse from ARQUES to No 10 Veterinary Hospital.	8

11th Mounted Vety Sect.

WAR DIARY
or
INTELLIGENCE SUMMARY.   N° 35

October 1918

Army Form C. 2118.

Hour, Date, Place		Summary of Events and Information	Remarks and references to Appendices
15 October	LE NIEPPE	Normal routine duties	
16 October	"	Evacuated sinus horse and one mule from AROVES Mob. Vety. Hospital	10
19 October	"	Collected one horse left by RHA belonging to ASC from M. DUQUESNE at STAPLE	1
20 October	"	Transferred his horse to Field Remount Section 2nd Army.	
21 October	"	Proceeded with 7th Cav. Bde. to FAUQUEMBERGUES	
22 October	FAUQUEMBERGUES	Went to FRUGES to attend conference of all V.O's 7th & 3rd Cav. Div.	
23 October	"	Inspected every horse BHQ Bty & Column for contagious disease, this took us greater part of day.	
25 October	"	Proceeded to FRUGES to take over temporary duties of A-DVS 3rd Cav. Div. in excess of my own duties.	

1/4 Lincolnshire Regt

Army Form C. 2118.

WAR DIARY
or
INTELLIGENCE SUMMARY.
(Erase heading not required.)

October 1915   No 36

Instructions regarding War Diaries and Intelligence Summaries are contained in F.S. Regs., Part II. and the Staff Manual respectively. Title pages will be prepared in manuscript.

Hour, Date, Place	Summary of Events and Information	Remarks and references to Appendices
25 October FAUQUEMBERGE	Proceeded eleven sick horses to Veterinary Hospital from LUMBRES	
26 October and FRUGES	Duties H.Q.t's with Convoy, in the afternoon taken Section outlie & remainder into FAUQUEMBERGE	
27 October to 31 October	the same duties.	

C. A. Jarvis
Capt. a/c
5/1 Lincoln Reg. Section.

WAR DIARY

OF

14th MOBILE VET. SECTION

3rd CAVALRY DIVISION

NOVEMBER + DECEMBER 1915

3 Cur
N

14th. Mrs. Van Sere.
Nov. + Dec. 1915.
Vol. IX XI

16 Middlesex Section

WAR DIARY November 1915. Army Form C. 2118.
or
INTELLIGENCE SUMMARY. No 37
(Erase heading not required.)

Hour, Date, Place	Summary of Events and Information	Remarks and references to Appendices
2 November. FAUQUEMBERGUE.	Evacuated to the 10 Cas Hosp from MIZERNES 16 cart horses and 8 sick horses	16 / 8
3 —	Received orders to forward wounded	
4 —	Greener Bloodwell. Pte A Brown Cpl Carr	
6 —	Arrived at FAUQUEMBERG, reported to Staff Captain 7th Cav Brig, & took over my duties from Capt Walker A.V.C. I reported to A.D.V.S. I received one horse from the 2nd Life Guards; suspicion skin, reported it to A.D.V.S Pte 15679 HE Luke arrived G.C.H. from No 2 Vety	
7 —	A.D.V.S. visited section in the morning. the remainder of the day occupied by sectional duties.	
8 —	A.D.V.S & D.D.V.S. visited the section at 8.30am with reference to a suspicious skin case of 1st Life Guards 1 suspicious skin case was evacuated from Wilsome to No 16 Vety Hospital.	1

114th Mobile Sec.   November 1915

Army Form C. 2118.

WAR DIARY
or
INTELLIGENCE SUMMARY.   No 38
(Erase heading not required.)

Instructions regarding War Diaries and Intelligence Summaries are contained in F.S. Regs., Part II. and the Staff Manual respectively. Title pages will be prepared in manuscript.

Hour, Date, Place	Summary of Events and Information	Remarks and references to Appendices
8 November. FAUQUEMBERGE.	I examined all horses of 114th Mob Sect, & nearly all of 7th Low Rang Hqrs. & Signal troop. Medical transferred G.C.H. 63 & 9 F.d. Fd Ambulance (exit only) O/C A.S.C. 6th Cav Field Ambulance.	
9	Sectional duties in the morning & attending sick cases of the Headquarters. 7 Cav Brig afternoon personally examined all the horses of R Batt R.H.A. & had no cases of suspicion mange or glanders. Sent off F.B122 & F.B39 F.d Medical who was transferred to 6 C.F.A. the previous day.	
10	Sectional duties in the morning. In the afternoon I examined all the horses of the 7th Cav Rang Headquarters.	
11.	Sectional duties in the morning. I examined all the horses of the 8th Cav Field Ambulance.	

14th North'n Sec. Nov 1916. No 39. Army Form C. 2118.

WAR DIARY
or
INTELLIGENCE SUMMARY.
(Erase heading not required.)

Hour, Date, Place	Summary of Events and Information	Remarks and references to Appendices
12 November FAUQVEMBERG	I paid out the men at 9.30. I evacuated if sick hutto from WIZERNES. 4 K. Baty R.H.A. 155 R.E. 17 Can F.A. 1.3 Can Du Hamp. 1 Nf&T Can Bring. they were accompanied by 1 Cafo & 1 man. Pinville A.D.V.S. I went to see the A.D.V.S at FRUGES in the afternoon. Pte Harvey reported sick, it was sent to Div Rest Camp.	
13 November FAUQUEMBERG	Sectional duties in the morning attending sick lines of Hd Qts 1st Can Bring. In the afternoon I went to K Battery R.H.A. to see the sick at DENNEBROEUCQ I went to find billets for the section in the morning. S of HERLY in the morning. C.A.D.R. came to FAUQVEMBE to see to employ nullers in the afternoon. Pte Nankle 1163 A.V.C. & Pte Smith 1283 A.V.C	
14		

14th Mobile Section

Nov 1915

No Sqa
H.Q.

Army Form C. 2118.

WAR DIARY
or
INTELLIGENCE SUMMARY.
(Erase heading not required.)

Hour, Date, Place	Summary of Events and Information	Remarks and references to Appendices
14 Nov FAUQUEMBERGE	reported here for duty from No 9 Vet Hosp Dieppe. Sent Pte Kennedy's B122 to O/c Base Remounts, he was reported to be at No 22 Casualty Clearing Station.	
15 —	Section duties in the morning. Pte Lott 22.the Hornwood & Pte Cooke were sent to the base, ostensibly A.D.V.S. the two horses to No 9 Vet Hosp. It later (noted) Horse. Invalid to Base R.H.A. developed a bad left detached my aggravated oedema of the chest & belly. 7 CAV BRIG moved from FAUQUEMBERGE to VERDURE. 14 M.V.S. moved at 9.15 a.m., roads very bad 3" of snow. Day taken up arranging billetting after mid day.	
16 — VERDURE		

11th Mobile Veterinary Section   Nov 1915.   Army Form C. 2118.

WAR DIARY
or
INTELLIGENCE SUMMARY.   No 44
(Erase heading not required.)

Hour, Date, Place	Summary of Events and Information	Remarks and references to Appendices
Nov 17. Verdrel.	Sectional duties in the morning. Two sections house of this section were attacked by the hounds. Veterinary authority D.A.D.R. found the headquarters in afternoon at Ternbery at Hucqueliers. To see sick horse. Down to 7 low field Ambulance at Bermont.	
— 18	Sectional duties all day. Examined all the horses of the section in the afternoon. I was visited by the D.D.V.S in the morning. Two lumber horses lame & below went to the 2nd Life Guards. Authority O.C.A.S.C. G.C.H.	
— 19	Sectional duties. I went to 20 M.V.S at Bermont.	
— 20	Sectional duties. Went to Hucqueliers to see headquarters 11C Bgde here, and BRIMONT to see 7th Cavalry Ambulance. Went to see A.D.V.S at FRUGES, from then to ASSONVAL to see 4 K Bty R.H.A. G.C.H.	
— 21	Sectional duties. Examined all the horses of 4 K Bty R.H.A. G.C.H.	

14th N.V.S.   Nov 19 16'

WAR DIARY
INTELLIGENCE SUMMARY.   No 4 How
(Erase heading not required.)

Army Form C. 2118.

Hour, Date, Place	Summary of Events and Information	Remarks and references to Appendices
Nov 22 VERDURE	Evacuated 7 sick men at MARESQUEL. I went then with 7 men, one Cpl, & interpreter. They went out to No 10 Vet Hosp in charge of our Cpl & our Pte. I lew Yeo, 2 and hyp [de 1 1st M/A Gde 17 C.F.A. I wired A.D.V.S. & O.C. No 10 Vet Hosp.	
— 23	Sectional duties, visited horses in Yeomanry at HERLY & WICQUINGHEM G.C.H.	
— 24	Visited horses Yeomanry in the morning. A.D.V.S. called him in the morning. Cpl. Helade informed him he duty from No 12 Vet Hospital. G.C.H.	
— 25	Visited horses Yeom at HERLY & WICQUINGHEM sick in a sanatorium show cases from N.Y. Afternoon went to FRUGES to see A.D.V.S.	
— 26	Visited A.D.V.S morning went to K Bty afternoon to see sick at ASSONVAL	

14 M.V.S.

Nov 1916
No 113

Army Form C. 2118.

WAR DIARY
or
INTELLIGENCE SUMMARY.

(Erase heading not required.)

Hour, Date, Place	Summary of Events and Information	Remarks and references to Appendices
Nov 27 VERDURE	Inspected A sqd hunter grooming at 10.45. the sqd from which suspicious skin case of yesterday was found. Pay am of 14 M.V.S. in afternoon. G.C.H.	
29	Visited hunter grooming in the morning at HERLY & WICQUINHEM. Sent usual duties in the morning, visited by A.D.V.S. in afternoon. G.C.H.	
30	Went to hunter grooming in morning at HERLY also to yard & horse lines & part of stud. Visited by A.D.V.S. & D.D.V.S. in afternoon. Closed for the month. G.C. Harding Capt. A.V.C.	

O.C. 14 M.V.S.

14 Mobile Veterinary Section

WAR DIARY
or
INTELLIGENCE SUMMARY.

December 1916.
No 4H.
Army Form C. 2118

Place	Date	Hour	Summary of Events and Information	Remarks and references to Appendices
VERDURÉ	1.12.16		Evacuated eight sick horses to 13 Vet Hosp. Received fifteen hundred francs from Paymaster 3rd Cav Div for Imprest Account. Visited K Bty R.H.A. now at ASSONVAL sick horse. Sick horse duties. G.C.H.	6
	2.12.16		Went to Lucheux Veterinary in morning saw to sick. Sat ordinary duties. Afternoon examined all horses of K Bty R.H.A. evening weekly returns. G.C.H. Standing	
	3.12.16		Attended horse Veterinary on parade by A.D.V.S. & D.V.S. in morning. Sat ordinary duties afternoon. Ph Veas & Phillingham at waggon horse lines G.C.H.	
	4.12.16		Went to ASSONVAL to meet A.D.V.S. & D.D.V.S. who inspected the K Bty R.H.A. horses. One case of Suspicion skin sent in to section from K Bty handed it out to A.D.V.S. Found Bty Vet 300 francs to send home G.C.H.	

WAR DIARY
or
INTELLIGENCE SUMMARY.

14 Mobile Veterinary Section   Dec 1916   Sheet No. H.9.

Army Form C. 2118

Place	Date	Hour	Summary of Events and Information	Remarks and references to Appendices
VERDUN	5.12.16		A.D.V.S. worked sick van in the morning. Sick van duties	
	6.12.16		Visited tenth Veterinary Sick van station. Pte Burton reported sick for duty.	G.C.H.
	4.12.16		Sick van duties	G.C.H.
	16.12.16		Went on leave from FEUGES	G.C.H.
	21.12.16		Returned from leave reported to A.D.V.S.	G.C.H.
	22.12.16		Inspected 1st Life Guards with Capt Watkin A.V.C. horses had mallanders. I injected all horses of 14 M.V.S. in a I know with mallein	G.C.H.
	23.12.16		Installed Nursery of K Bty for glanders. Reported A.D.V.S.	G.C.H.
	24.12.16		Received am order of K Bty d Ahem be attached temporarily some down daytime to 14 M.V.S. Found men 14 M.V.S.	

14 Mobile Veterinary Section

WAR DIARY
or
INTELLIGENCE SUMMARY.
(Erase heading not required.)

Army Form C. 2118
Dec 1915.
Sheet No A6.

Place	Date	Hour	Summary of Events and Information	Remarks and references to Appendices
Verdure	25.12.15		Inspected K Bty horse at ASSONVAL ordered him inflated with hallein, salvin dulin.	
	26.12.15		Inspected horses 1st Bty at TRIMEUX & men of Ammunition Column. Went to Bde Hqs to see S.O. & I.O. managed coal. GOURAY.	
	27.12.15		Met A.D.V.S. at GOURAY to see sun burn case of X Bty. It was sent to the section A.D.V.S. Cav Corps inspected sun burn case him at night. Went to X weeks to see A.D.V.S. at 7.30 pm.	
	28.12.15		Went to Bde Hqs to see Staff Capt for information re discipline at HUCQUELIERS. Afternoon met Capt Richardson at FRUGES re hatching gun horses	
	29.12.15		changes Went to lunch hors in morning. 1.30 inspected all horses with wallein with Capt Wallworker	
	30.12.15		inspected horses of hospital premium with A.D.V.S. on that been held	
	31.12.15		Afternoon washed K Bty at ASSONVAL. Inspected hospital premium with A.D.V.S. visited K Bty in afternoon at ASSONVAL close	

G.C. Harding
Capt. A.V.C. O.C. 14 M.V.S.

14th Mobile Veterinary Section

WAR DIARY — January 1916
INTELLIGENCE SUMMARY. NO App.

Army Form C. 2118.

Place	Date	Hour	Summary of Events and Information	Remarks and references to Appendices
VERDURE	1.1.16		Inspected horse kunsha yeomanry which had been maltreated into falphal maltod with ADVS Cavalry. ADVS & later Div visited 12 suspect. I took in 2 sick pneumonia cases to 14MVS from kunsha yeomanry, also (Knur suspected two) from which above named section now in evacuation.	12
	2.1.16		Went to FRUGES. Saw charges of Capt Richardson A.V.C.	2
	3.1.16		Went to FRUGES. Inspected 6 horses (intra falphal maltod) of Aux horse transport coy.	6
	4.1.16		A.S.C. school duties. Sectional duties.	
	5.1.16		Evacuated 28 sick horses at MONTREVIL. Went to ADVS.	
	6.1.16		morning. Went round kunsha yeomanry in morning. Went to see half section at HUCQUISE 15-RS in afternoon.	
	7.1.16		Sectional duties & visited hunsha yeomanry.	
	8.1.16		Recovered two horses through kunsha yeomanry. ADVS came over to section.	
	9.1.16		kunsha yeomanry in morning. Drove bay horse in a stream	
	10.1.16		ADVS & Cav Infy ADVS & later Div Inspection kunsha of kunsha hunsha kunsha of yeomanry. I had over the command of the section.	

1st Mobile Veterinary Section

WAR DIARY or **INTELLIGENCE SUMMARY**

Army Form C. 2118.

January 1916
NO xx6

Place	Date	Hour	Summary of Events and Information	Remarks and references to Appendices
VERDURE	11.1.16		Went to Hussar Yeomanry in morning at WICQUINHEM, & 2nd Life Guards in afternoon	
	12.1.16		Sat on a dentition wounded 2 sore-backs mange case from Hussar Yeomanry. Visited by ADVS, went to gather the result of mange army. Three acetabulum chair case.	2
	13.1.16		Went to Hussar Yeomanry in morning in afternoon of horse taken here of the section. ADVS called here	
	14.1.16		Went to Hussar Yeomanry in morning. Sent old man to 3rd DGs until 2nd DADR Cav Bdgs. Later went to 2nd Life Guards at HUCQUELIERS	
	15.1.16	—	Made P.M. on mare of K Bty RHA. Inadequate nodules in lung implied. 12 here. Thence Yeomanry in afternoon.	
	16.1.16	—	Inspected horses of Hussar Yeomanry inspected previous day. Employed another mare down day. Wife sent out to Hufflatten lung 103.0 afternoon is damned veterinary cases at 2nd Life Guards	
	17.1.16	—	Examined veterinary cases of section for evening. Examined one from glanders cases at Hussars undergoing the test	

11th K Noble Yeomanry Section   January 1919

WAR DIARY or INTELLIGENCE SUMMARY. No. 9

Army Form C. 2118.

Place	Date	Hour	Summary of Events and Information	Remarks and references to Appendices
VERDURE	18-1-19		Examined 13 horses of Cavalry Tramway under the mallein test. Returned of A.s.qd horses.	13
	19-1-19		Examined 16 horses from MONTREVIL	16
			At HERLY 3 horses destroyed. Amount of mallein test P.M. showed glanders. A.D.V.S & N Davis were present	3
	20-1-19		Inspected A squadron Cavalry Tramway, afternoon sick on duties	
	21-1-19		Attended casting parade at Hucecliers Cavalry Tramway headquarters, sick on duties afternoon	
	22-1-19		Sick on duties in morning afternoon examined 10 remount horses at Hucecliers ceremony	10
	23-1-19		Morning went to HUCQUELIERS to see about kit for sick on afternoon went to FERGNY & Ind & HHK.	
	24-1-19		Submitted return A.D.V.S called to inspect horse for evacuation afternoon went to FRUGES to get report, morning to Ferg now 1500 horses. Hard Kind at 6pm.	
	25-1-19		Evacuated 3 sick cases escorted by D.A.D.R C.16 yesterday goes at MONTREVIL	
	26-1-19		Went to HICQVINGHEM in morning to Hucecliers Tramway afternoon to see A.D.V.S & Staff	
	27-1-19		Captain Kent removes about a pencil	
	28-1-19		Went to see Hd Qts Vere Staff Capt sick on duties	
	29-1-19		Awarded 28 days fuel Punished to be to go to forall, went to Hucecliers Tramway	

1st Northern/Sy Sullers.

WAR DIARY
or
INTELLIGENCE SUMMARY.
(Erase heading not required.)

Army Form C. 2118.

January 1916
No 50

Place	Date	Hour	Summary of Events and Information	Remarks and references to Appendices
VERDURE	29.1.16		Sent 16 hundred groom in the morning By Togoob. Yerad to was sent to A.P.M. at Duvin and held grades to integrate Jumna head. Afternoon went to see S.O. 17 Cav Bde.	
	30.1.16		Sat work duties.	
	31.1.16		Sat work duties.	

Closed for the month.

G. L. Harding.
Capt. a R.C.

WAR DIARY or INTELLIGENCE SUMMARY

Army Form C. 2118.

14th Mobile Veterinary Section

February 1916

Instructions regarding War Diaries and Intelligence Summaries are contained in F.S. Regs., Part II. and the Staff Manual respectively. Title pages will be prepared in manuscript.

Place	Date	Hour	Summary of Events and Information	Remarks and references to Appendices
VERDURE	1.2.16		Sectional duties	
	2.2.16		Sectional duties A.D.V.S. called	
	3.2.16		Visited Hucqueliers Yeomanry went to look at billets for sick coy at BELLE VUE in afternoon	
	4.2.16		Visited Hucqueliers Yeomanry in morning, sectional duties	
	5.2.16		Visited Hucqueliers Yeomanry in morning, went to FRUGES & car A.D.V.S. 3 horses were treated in the night with mallein of Hucqueliers Yeomanry	
	6.2.16		Sex annually their horses at Hucqueliers Yeomanry tested twice a day with mallein. Drew 560 francs from Paymaster Boulogne A.D.V.S. came to HERLY to see these horses tested & inspected the Capt	
	7.2.16		Walked to AVC in afternoon went to HUCQUELIERS B Sqn S.O. reported the 14th Mobile Veterinary Section moved from VERDURE outbreak	
	8.2.16		Staff Capt Afternoon U DV 5 Cav Lubgs AA DVS 3D Cav Div visited section at BELLE VUE examined these skin cases	
BELLEVUE	9.2.16		Visited troops at FRUGES in morning, Bouland in afternoon Eural & APK at Hucqueliers Yeomanry at HUCQUELIERS. WICQUINGHEM	

14 K N able Valenwayn Soldier   February
                                                  No 52

WAR DIARY
or
INTELLIGENCE SUMMARY
(Erase heading not required.)

Army Form C. 2118.

Instructions regarding War Diaries and Intelligence
Summaries are contained in F. S. Regs., Part II.
and the Staff Manual respectively. Title pages
will be prepared in manuscript.

Place	Date	Hour	Summary of Events and Information	Remarks and references to Appendices
BELLE VUE	10.2.16		Evacuated our sick horses & three other cases at MONTREVIL visited branches yesterday	6 - 3
			at HUCQUELIERS.	
	11.2.16		Visited DIV TROOPS at FRUGES in morning. Several sick in afternoon	
	12.2.16		Went to VERDURE with A.D.V.S. in morning & saw suspicious skin cases of	2
			Household Yeomanry. P.H. Reps. A.V.C. all visited, form duty with the 3rd Dismounted	
			Squadron.	
	13.2.16		Several duties	
	14.2.16		Several duties in the morning, afternoon went to FRUGES to see Div Troops	
	15.2.16		A.D.V.S & D.D.V.S. inspected sick cases at VERDURE front to AVCQUELIERS	
			in afternoon to Household Yeomanry	
	16.2.16		Visited Household Yeomanry in the morning, examined their skin cases, went to	
			Div troops in afternoon at FRUGES.	
	17.2.16		Visited Household Yeomanry in the morning inspected No 2 kemp. Hurst to Rennes	
			& saw farrier who does all labors for pushed unit of H&B squadrons. Several	
			duties in the afternoon	
	18.2.16		Several duties in the morning, in the afternoon I visited Div armed troops	

WAR DIARY
or
INTELLIGENCE SUMMARY

Army Form C. 2118.

(Erase heading not required.)

1/1 K N ddl Yeomanry Bde

February No 58

Place	Date	Hour	Summary of Events and Information	Remarks and references to Appendices
BELLEVUE	19.2.16		Visited the Bucks Yeomanry in the morning. The A.D.V.S. + D.V.S. inspected the sad cow in the afternoon. They (C) went to VERDURE with me to see suspicious skin cases.	
	20.2.16		Sanitary duties in the morning, in the afternoon inspected some horses at Khuricchur Yeomanry.	
	21.2.16		Visited Khuricchur Yeomanry, went with the A.D.V.S. in the morning, in the afternoon I went to draw money to pay the men from Paymaster 2nd Cav Dn at FRUGES.	
	22.2.16		Went to No 13 M.V.S. with the A.D.V.S.	
	23.2.16		Sanitary duties, in the morning, in the afternoon I went to FRUGES to see A.P.M. to arrange about the transport of Yorself who was under punishment at the division.	
	24.2.16		Visited the Bucks Yeomanry in the morning, with the A.D.V.S & D.D.V.S. to look at some suspicious skin cases. In the afternoon I went to the Khuricchur Yeomanry.	
	25.2.16		Visited Buckinghamshire company in the morning, railway arrival duties. On Yorself who I transferred to No 3 Cav Field Ambulance	

1st Notts Volunteer Coy Stolow

WAR DIARY
or
INTELLIGENCE SUMMARY.

Army Form C. 2118.

February 1915

Place	Date	Hour	Summary of Events and Information	Remarks and references to Appendices
BELLE VUE	26.2.16		Morning I went to Juvincourt American Column returned sectional duties	
	27.2.16		Visited Hautebraye gun coy in the morning, afternoon sectional duties	
	28.2.16		Visited Hautebraye gun coy with the Adj't N.S in the morning sectional duties in the afternoon	
	29.2.16		Visited Juvincourt American Column in the morning sectional duties in the afternoon	
			Closed for the month	

G C Harding
Capt a.V.C.
O.C. 1st Hertfordshire Coy

11th Mobile Veterinary Section

WAR DIARY
or
INTELLIGENCE SUMMARY.

March
Sheet No 5

Army Form C. 2118.

(Erase heading not required.)

Instructions regarding War Diaries and Intelligence Summaries are contained in F. S. Regs., Part II. and the Staff Manual respectively. Title pages will be prepared in manuscript.

Place	Date	Hour	Summary of Events and Information	Remarks and references to Appendices
BELLEVUE	1.3.16		Evacuated eight sick horses at Montreuil & one suspicious skin case. Visited Hucqueliers & Yacomanien	%1
	2.3.16		ADVS inspected suspicious skin cases at Hucqueliers. Yeomanry received duties in the morning	
	3.3.16		Sectional duties in the morning. Visited Hucqueliers Yeomanry in the afternoon	
	4.3.16		Sectional duties. ADVS inspected certain marching order & medical inspection. Drove in the afternoon	
	5.3.16		Drew 2,000 francs from the Paymaster 2nd Cav Div to pay the men. Pte Jennings attached to the section for duty.	
	6.3.16		ADVS visited the section in the morning, inspected skin cases at the Hucqueliers Yeomanry. Paid men in the afternoon	
	7.3.16		Went to Hucqueliers Yeomanry in the morning sectional duties in the afternoon.	
	8.3.16		Visited K Bty in the morning (advisory) visit of ice to A.D.V.S.	
	9.3.16		Visited Hucqueliers Yeomanry in the morning sectional duties in the afternoon	
	10.3.16		Visited McQUINCHEM HUCQUELIERS in the morning to meet ADVS & DDVS & inspect skin cases also skin cases at Hucqueliers Yeomanry at VERDURE	

11th Mobile Veterinary Section

WAR DIARY
or
INTELLIGENCE SUMMARY.

Sheet No 56

Army Form C. 2118.

(Erase heading not required.)

Instructions regarding War Diaries and Intelligence Summaries are contained in F. S. Regs., Part II. and the Staff Manual respectively. Title pages will be prepared in manuscript.

Place	Date	Hour	Summary of Events and Information	Remarks and references to Appendices
BELLE VUE	11-3-16		Sectional duties. I went to Bde HdQts to see S.O. at HUCQUELIERS.	
	12-3-16		Sectional duties	
	13-3-16		A.D.V.S. visited skin cases at VERDURE and WICQUINGHEM sectional duties.	
	14-3-16		11th Mobile Veterinary Section moved into new billet at AVESNES	
AVESNES	15-3-16		Visited K Bty R.H.A at ASSONVAL	
	16-3-16		Visited Hucqueliere Veterinary sectional duties	
	17-3-16		A.D.V.S. visited the section sectional duties in the morning	
	18-3-16		Visited Hucqueliere Veterinary included Csquadron sectional duties in the afternoon	
	19-3-16		Sectional duties examined horses for remount of C squadron Hucqueliere Yeomanry went to see S.O. Bde Hd Qts in afternoon	
	20-3-16		A.D.V.S visited the section I drove 1400 lb bus from Dr Payne who said DW at FRUGES in afternoon to lay the man.	
	21-3-16		Sectional duties in the morning I went to K Bty R.H.A. in the afternoon	
	22-3-16		Went to Hucqueliere Yeo in the morning of sectional duties in the afternoon.	
	23-3-16		Sectional duties	
	24-3-16		Sectional duties in the morning went to K Bty R.H.A in afternoon vaccinated all the mess	

1st Mobile Veterinary Section

WAR DIARY
or
INTELLIGENCE SUMMARY.

Army Form C. 2118.

March   Sheet No 5.

Place	Date	Hour	Summary of Events and Information	Remarks and references to Appendices
AVESNES	25.3.16	—	Sectional duties in the morning. A.D.V.S. called. No remounts arrived in the afternoon to investigate horse army.	
	26.3.16	—	Examined No remounts again with various squadrons.	
	27.3.16	—	A.D.V.S. called to see horses & examine sectional duties in the afternoon.	
	28.3.16	—	Examined 2 sick horses at MONTREUIL visited R.Bty. R.H.A. removed two humours from the hogs. Had to put down sectional duties in the afternoon.	
	29.3.16	—	Sectional duties, examined B squadron Horse army, sectional duties in the afternoon	
	30.3.16	—	Sectional duties in the morning afternoon with inspection ammunition, went for walk. Saw A.D.V.S. he put them cases.	
	31.3.16	—	A.D.V.S. called to see other cases at HERLY in the morning, sectional duties in afternoon	
			Closed for the month.	

G.C. Standing
Capt. A.V.C.
O.C. 1st M.V.S.

1st Noble Yeomanry Section

WAR DIARY or INTELLIGENCE SUMMARY

April 1916
Sheet No 59.

Army Form C. 2118.

Place	Date	Hour	Summary of Events and Information	Remarks and references to Appendices
AVESNES	1.4.16		Ed examined A squadron Hurshishin Yeomanry, & sub of B&C squadrons. voted K Bty in the afternoon, vet'nal duties	
	2.4.16		Vet'nal duties men attended church parade at HERLY	
	3.4.16		ADVS visited the section. I took in H. skin case from the Hunslishin Yeomanry and two men to look after them. vet'nal duties in the afternoon	4
	4.4.16		Examined 3 skin cases and 15 sick horses from MONTREUIL, visited Hunslishin Yeomanry skBty RHA	3, 15
	5.4.16		Vet'nal duties	
	6.4.16		My horse granted by ADVS 3rd Cav Div commenced. Capt Walker took charge of my duties	
	6.4.16		Returned to duty from leave	
	9.4.16		Vet'nal duties. 17th armed horse at B squadron Hunslishin Yeomanry	
	10.4.16		ADVS called to see horses for wound row, I sent away three skin cases from B squadron Hunslishin Yeomanry these 500 paces from Paymaster 3rd Cav Div	3
	11.4.16		Vet'nal duties I went to H squadron Hunslishin Yeomanry	

WAR DIARY

1st Nottinghamshire Section.

April 1916

INTELLIGENCE SUMMARY. 2nd No 6 a.

Army Form C. 2118.

Place	Date	Hour	Summary of Events and Information	Remarks and references to Appendices
AVESNES	18.4.16		Sedimental duties. Went to B squadron Hundschin Yeomanry	
	19.4.16		Visited B squadron and C squadron hundschin Yeomanry also headquarters	
	20.4.16		sedimental duties	
			Sedimental duties visited K Bty R.H.A. in afternoon	
	21.4.16		Sedimental duties. Saw the cut of hundschin Yeomanry examined the teeth of B squadron in the afternoon	
	22.4.16		Sedimental duties	
	23.4.16		Examined A squadron and horses sedimental duties	
	24.4.16		A.D.V.S. called to see the sick horses in A & B squadron in the morning	
	25.4.16		Examined A squadron hundschin Yeomanry sedimental duties	
	26.4.16		Sedimental duties, attended the divisional box long show	
	27.4.16		Cpl Wolle at his own request reverted the rank of private, L/Cpl Welding to be promoted in his place (approved A.D.V.S. 20 Cav Div) examined K Bty R.H.A. in the afternoon	
	28.4.16		Saw the cut of hundschin Yeomanry sedimental duties	
	29.4.16		Examined remounts of C squadron, sedimental duties with and	

WAR DIARY
or
INTELLIGENCE SUMMARY.

(Erase heading not required.)

Army Form C. 2118.

1st Mobile Veterinary Section   April 1916   Sheet No 61

Place	Date	Hour	Summary of Events and Information	Remarks and references to Appendices
AVESNES	29th 30.4.16		Sunday inspection at 3.30 heated thoroughly harness & removed cat cases and ailments of H.Q. & squadron. Closed for the month. G. C. Harding Capt. A.V.C.	

Army Form C. 2118.

D/H Noble Veterinary Sergeon. WAR DIARY or INTELLIGENCE SUMMARY. May 1916. Sheet No 62.

Instructions regarding War Diaries and Intelligence Summaries are contained in F. S. Regs., Part II. and the Staff Manual respectively. Title pages will be prepared in manuscript.

May 1916

Place	Date	Hour	Summary of Events and Information	Remarks and references to Appendices
AVESNES	1.5.16		Sectional duties. A.D.V.S. called in the morning, visited K.B.Ey in the afternoon	
	2.5.16		Evacuated 1 mange case, 5 sick horses, visited the Leicester Yeomanry.	
	3.5.16		Sectional duties	
	4.5.16		Sectional duties, visited Leicestershire Yeomanry and KBEy	
	5.5.16		Sectional duties	
HUCQUELIERS	6.5.16		Sectional moved from AVESNES to HUCQUELIERS.	
	7.5.16		Visited the Machine Gun Squadron at AIX en ERGNY sectional duties	
	8.5.16		A.D.V.S. called to see the section, visited the Leicestershire Yeomanry, 1st Life Guards and 2nd Life Guards.	
	9.5.16		Sectional duties	
	10.5.16		Examined H.Q. of 7th Cav Bde and 9th Cav Field Ambulance, Sectional duties, saw the A.D.V.S. at night.	
	11.5.16		Examined Leicestershire Yeomanry sick and 2nd Life Guards sick, sectional duties	
	12.5.16		Sectional duties. Prepared for the move on following day	

Army Form C. 2118.

WAR DIARY
or
INTELLIGENCE SUMMARY.

May 1916
Sheet No 63.

(Erase heading not required.)

Instructions regarding War Diaries and Intelligence Summaries are contained in F.S. Regs., Part II. and the Staff Manual respectively. Title pages will be prepared in manuscript.

Place	Date	Hour	Summary of Events and Information	Remarks and references to Appendices
LE PLOUY	13.5.16		1st K Noble Yeomanry Section moved from HUCQUELIERS to LE PLOUY one mile No 1 of N. FRESSIN starting at 6.30 am and arriving at 12.30 pm under its own arrangements.	
			Part of the section was lodging at mounted officers and 18 men and 20 horses and a billet it turns and 4 men was left which gave rather over strength at HUCQUELIERS with billets B.	
			The deed four horses over to the 20 M.V.S at RIMBOVAL to carry through 1st Life Guards 1XR Hy Among the much it rained increasingly. All men and horses were put under cover for the night - rain rations were drawn at CAVRON	
ST MARTIN	14.5.16		The day was spent cleaning horses and harness.	
	15.5.16		Reveille at 4 am horses watered and fed at 4.30. the section marched to FRESSIN where it fell in behind 1st Life Guards Echelon, & marched continuously and very heavily. Echelon halted at FROYELLES to water and feed.	
			The section arrived at L'HEVRE arriving at 2.30 pm the roads the day were wyred really all the way by had miles of grit which added greatly to friction	

WAR DIARY
or
INTELLIGENCE SUMMARY.

1st Mobile Veterinary Section

Army Form C. 2118.

Place	Date	Hour	Summary of Events and Information	Remarks and references to Appendices
	15.5.16		and examined the wear of shoes, feet of the horses was fair, I found all horses and men under cover and found good water. General Howe passed by the section	
L'HEUVE	16.5.16		Visited 2nd Life Guards to see Capt Wuthen AVC, re making of units. No 10 a.d.s. was new dug and good. Sectional duties visited 1st Life Guards at night	
	17.5.16		ADMS visited the section, I visited the 1st Life Guards, K Bty and 1st C Field Ambulance. I called to see a lame case at 1st C Field Ambulance at night	
	18.5.16		Received horses for evacuation and took them to No 22 Vety Hospital ABBEVILLE	
	19.5.16		Went to 1st Life Guards and K Bty and 1st Cav Field Ambulance to arrange for the evacuation of sick	
	20.5.16		Received no horses from X R Hus, 1st Cav Field Ambulance. I evacuated 10 horses to No 22 ABBEVILLE general duties.	
	21.5.16		Marched to LABROYE starting at 6 am, followed up by 1st Life Guards	

WAR DIARY
or
INTELLIGENCE SUMMARY

14 Mobile Veterinary Sec. Army Form C. 2118.
Sheet 6/5

Place	Date	Hour	Summary of Events and Information	Remarks and references to Appendices
			horses at CAOURS and 6 men left our horse lines with Nos Carpentier The section then marched to X roads west of NEUILLY L'HOPITAL & arrived there by 9 am. the Section up to 2nd Life Guard horse l[ines] & handed [over] horse[s] sick with 3 men it 3 orders I marched on and did Marchéville at 11.30. lunched on and entered LABROYE at 2 pm and took over 2nd Life Guards sick own riders and one man but said our horses unable to use the other on used ground	
	22/5/16		left LABROYE at 6.45 am and trekked to HESDIN [via?] NOT HUBY Sthen had to destroy one of 2nd Life Guards horses it was taken with violent symptoms of colic and unable to did. I arranged for its disposal in HESDIN and came to at FRESSIN at 12.30. Axe & all horses up watered and fed	
	23/5/16		left FRESSIN at 9 am had to leave a horse behind at SAINS LES FRESSIN as it was unable to more went 1st Life Guards, I handed over 11 horses 3 men Ill. Life Guards 2nd Life Guards to sick horses and 1 man and one rider at RIMBOVAL I took housekeeping from my sub on to	

WAR DIARY
or
INTELLIGENCE SUMMARY.
(Erase heading not required.)

Army Form C. 2118.

Sheet 66. 1. Mobile Veterinary Section

Place	Date	Hour	Summary of Events and Information	Remarks and references to Appendices
HVCQVELIERS			HVCQVELIERS anunagnl 12.30 p.m. I still had such horses 2/3 motice to handed in from army at BOVRTES I visited horse section from army and 2nd Life Guards my afternoon when when when to see MUC	
	24.5.16		inspected the Lan Duke Md OC lines, attended parade of our tank cases by Brigadier major of Lincolnshire Yeomanry from 11 a.m. – 1.30 p.m. Visited HQ & two of Lincolnshire Yeomanry in the afternoon Visited Lincolnshire Yeomany all squadrons attended to sick and three of our veterinary sergeant duties	
	26.5.16		Sent in weekly return visited 1st Life Guards sick & cases of evacuation was called to see cases at Lincolnshire Yeomanry in the evening	
	27.5.16		2K N015200 Boom reported here for duty. Helped to remove a horse of Lincolnshire Yeomanry that had fallen into a well. I visited later all the horse	
	28.5.16		Visited 7th Machine Gun Squadron & found two cases for evacuation	

WAR DIARY
or
INTELLIGENCE SUMMARY.

1st Mobile Veterinary Section
Sheet 69
Army Form C. 2118.

(Erase heading not required.)

Instructions regarding War Diaries and Intelligence Summaries are contained in F. S. Regs., Part II. and the Staff Manual respectively. Title pages will be prepared in manuscript.

Place	Date	Hour	Summary of Events and Information	Remarks and references to Appendices
HVC. AUBIGNY	1ST to 29TH		Sergeant Clarke to remain investigating Yeomanry & 1st Life Guards	Q. 1.
			4th Madras Gun Squadron, 1 Mange film 1st Life Guards	2.
			Visited Household Yeomanry & received a few wounded horses	
			Received on the previous day.	
	30.6.16			
	31.5.16		Examined the dispatch horses, 4th Cav. Field Ambulance, sectional duties typed the men	
			Used for the month	
			G. L. Harding	
			Capt. A.V.C.	

WAR DIARY
or
INTELLIGENCE SUMMARY.
(Erase heading not required.)

14 Mobile Veterinary Sec... Army Form C. 2118.

Sheet 6 ?

June 1916

Place	Date	Hour	Summary of Events and Information	Remarks and references to Appendices
HUQUELIERS	1.6.16		Visited hecestaches Yeomanry in the morning, sectional duties	
	2.6.16		Sectional duties, visited hecestaches Yeomanry	
	3.6.16		Sectional duties, visited hecestaches Yeomanry	
	4.6.16		Sectional duties, visited hecestaches Yeomanry	
	5.6.16		A.D.V.S. called & saw horses for evacuation in the morning. Visited hecestaches Yeomanry	
	6.6.16		Evacuated horses to hecestaches Yeomanry. 1 BdeH.Q.G., 1st Life Guards. Manage visited hecestaches Yeomanry and examined H. mount	5.L.G.
	7.6.16		Examined Bde H.Q.G., 1st Life Guards. 1st Law Field Ambulance sectional duties, I went & saw A.D.V.S.	
	8.6.16		Sectional duties, visited hecestaches Yeomanry	
	9.6.16		Sectional duties	
	10.6.16		Sectional duties	
	11.6.16		Sectional duties visited the out of H.Qrs. headquarters	
	12.6.16		Yesterday Both H.Q.G., A.D.V.S. called at the section	
	13.6.16		Sectional duties, visited sick at Bgade headquarters.	

WAR DIARY
or
INTELLIGENCE SUMMARY.

(Erase heading not required.)

Army Form C. 2118.

1st Mobile Veterinary Section O.C.

Place	Date	Hour.	Summary of Events and Information	Remarks and references to Appendices
HUCQUELIERS	14-6-16		Examined head quarters and 7th Car Shed Ambulance	
	15-6-16		Sectional duties, visited the MDQT sick	
	16-6-16		Received cases for evacuation, visited headquarters sick	
	17-6-16		Evacuated 2 slim cases of 1st Life Guards, 15 sick & 6 cast cases	2,13,5.
	18-6-16		Sectional duties	
	19-6-16		Examined HQQE sectional duties	
	20-6-16		Examined Bde MDQt sick sectional duties	
	21-6-16		Sectional duties examined sick of Bde Hd Qts	
	22-6-16		A.D.V.S. called, evacuated return case of 2nd Life Guards, 15" sick, and 1 cast to M.V.S.	1,15 1.
	23-6-16		Sectional duties, packing up for move in the next day	
	24-6-16		Moved from HUCQUELIERS to WARDICOURT (starting at 4.30 pm and arriving at 5.30 am)	
	25-6-16		Moved from WARDICOURT to BEAUMART LES DAMES starting at 4.30 pm and arriving at 4.30 am	
	26-6-16		Moved from WARDICOURT to BONNAY starting at 4.30 pm arrived at	

June 1916   Sheet 6/9   Army Form C. 2118.

WAR DIARY
or
INTELLIGENCE SUMMARY.

Mobile Veterinary Section

(Erase heading not required.)

Place	Date	Hour	Summary of Events and Information	Remarks and references to Appendices
BONNAY	27.6.16		12 Sgn. & Farrier continuously sent in horses in a most satisfactory conditions. A.D.V.S called	
	28.6.16		Evacuated horses from H.Q. 7 Cav. Bn. H.S. in all from two brigades at MERRICOURT & Hoy VETY HOSPITAL at FORGES LES EAUX, visited sick at Both Bd. QG.	
	29.6.16		Sectional duties visited Both Bd QGs sick	
	30.6.16		Handed 1 horse of H.Q. Bd. Amm Column to 20th M.V.S. sectional duties visited sick at Bde HQ QL.	

Award for the month

C. L. Harding
Capt. AVC.

WAR DIARY or INTELLIGENCE SUMMARY

Army Form C. 2118.

July 1916 — sheet 71 — 14 Mobile Veterinary Section

Vol 17

Place	Date	Hour	Summary of Events and Information	Remarks and references to Appendices
BONNAY	1.7.16		Sectional duties, section stood to at 7.30 am eventually we did not move. Visited Bde HQ.	
	2.7.16		Sectional duties visited Bde HQ & HQ of 7th Can Fried Ambulance	
	3.7.16		Sectional duties visited Bde HQ and 7th Can Field Ambulance	
	4.7.16		Stood to at 6.30 am and moved from BONNAY to WANEL arrived about 9 pm	
WANEL	5.7.16		Sectional duties, attended the sale of 7th Pack Machine Gun Section ad Bde Horses	
	6.7.16		A.D.V.S. visited. The sale was approved subject to evacuation. Evacuated 9 sick horses and 1 skin case to No 22 Vety Hospital ABBEVILLE. Section stood to from 6.30 am and was ready to move at 15 hrs notice.	
	7.7.16		Evacuated 12 sick horses to No 22 ABBEVILLE left one horse of 7th Machine Gun Squadron hereths the treasurary at WANEL suffering from laminitis.	
	8.7.16		Section moved in the afternoon to CORBIE arriving at 7.30 am	
CORBIE	9.7.16		Bivouacked in a meadow at CORBIE sectional duties	
	10.7.16		Sectional duties	

July 1916   Sheet 72   Army Form C. 2118.

WAR DIARY
or
INTELLIGENCE SUMMARY. D.H.Q Mobile Veterinary Section

(Erase heading not required.)

Place	Date	Hour	Summary of Events and Information	Remarks and references to Appendices
CORBIE	10-7-16		Sectional duties	
"	11-7-16		Sectional duties	
"	12-7-16		Evacuated 9 sick horses and 3 mange cases at MERRICOURT	
"	13-7-16		Ordered to stand to at 11 am	
"	14-7-16		Sectional duties should be ready to move	
"	15-7-16		Sectional duties	
"	16-7-16		Sectional duties, one horse was destroyed 17th Bde Ammn Column	
"	17-7-16		Sectional duties, one horse was transferred to 20 Mobile Veterinary Section	
"	18-7-16		Sectional duties	
"	19-7-16		One horse of 13 VB 2nd an Div was sent to 20 Mobile Veterinary Section	
"	20-7-16		Sectional duties attended 7th CFA and BDQS	
"	21-7-16		Sectional duties attended 7th CFA and BDQS	
"	22-7-16		Sectional duties attended 7th CFA and BDQS	
"	23-7-16		Visited Bde HQ QS and 7th CFA sectional duties	
"	24-7-16		Sectional duties one horse BBdy RCA returned to duty	
"	25-7-16		Sectional duties	

WAR DIARY
or
INTELLIGENCE SUMMARY.

Army Form C. 2118.

July 1916 Sheet 73

Pk N Mobile Veterinary Section

Place	Date	Hour	Summary of Events and Information	Remarks and references to Appendices
CORBIE	26.7.16		Sectional duties, attended BHQ & Officer of Advance	
	27.7.16		Sectional duties. One horse of Officers Field Ambulance transferred to the 20th Mobile Veterinary Section	
	28.7.16		Sectional duties	
	29.7.16		Sectional duties	
	30.7.16		Sectional duties	
	31.7.16		Mr Hayes was awarded to hospital by Veterinary Hospital. Chestnut pony of Capt Smalley I.M.S. attended to daily and sent to Convalescent Depot this Record ready to be ready to be on move at 6.30 am the next morning.	

Diary closed for the month

G. C. Shading

Capt A.V.C.

WAR DIARY or INTELLIGENCE SUMMARY

14 Mobile Veterinary Section Sheet of 4. Army Form C. 2118.

August 1916

Place	Date	Hour	Summary of Events and Information	Remarks and references to Appendices
CORBIE	1.8.16		Marched to OISSY arriving at 2 o'clock p.m. Included one mare from CONVILLE belonging to the Australian Staff Ammn Colun, we bivouacked for the night.	
OISSY	2.8.16		Marched to DRUCY started at 5:30 a.m. and arrived at 2:30 p.m. Left a horse of the Machine Gun Squadron at PIENCOURT near O.F. base H.Q. at	
DRUCY	3.8.16		Sectional duties visited Huestrehu Yeomanry and Bde H.Q at	
DRUCY	4.8.16		Evacuated 9 sick horses to No 22 ABLEVILLE from St RIGQUIERS. Marched to AREOULES arrived at 12 a.m. afterwards bivouacked for the night.	
AREOULES	5.8.16		Marched from DRUCY to AVEQUELIERS arrived at 10:45 a.m. and entered old billet.	
AVEQUELIERS	6.8.16		Sectional duties visited H.O.O.G. and Huestrehu Yeomanry.	
	7.8.16		Sectional duties A.D.V.S called.	
	8.8.16		Evacuated 27 sick horses to No 13 Vety HOSPITAL	
	9.8.16		Examined Bde H.d Qts, visited Huestrehu Yeomanry sectional duties	
	10.8.16		Sectional duties rode my unit	
	11.8.16		Went to Huestrehu Yeomanry Bde H.Q G., d/Col h/q Grade to arrange about take over some mange cases	

WAR DIARY
or
INTELLIGENCE SUMMARY.

17th Mobile Veterinary Section

Sheet 75.
August 1916

Army Form C. 2118.

Place	Date	Hour	Summary of Events and Information	Remarks and references to Appendices
HULQUELIERS	13.8.16	—	Sectional duties worked to HQ 95 elsewhere the Yeomanry	
	10.8.16	—	Sectional duties	
	12.8.16	—	Sectional duties. A.D.V.S called to visit the sub-lines for evacuation	
	15.8.16	—	Evacuated 10 sub-horses to Horse Vety Hospital NEUFCHATEL	
	16.8.16	—	Examined 11 horses of 80th HQ 95 and 1st CFA.	
	17.8.16	—	A field General Court Martial was held on SE 13556 Pte Hughes H.V.S. of the sub-lines. He was awarded 14 days F.P. No. 1. Sectional duties	
	18.8.16	—	Sectional duties, promulgated the sentence of SE 13556 Pte Hughes H.V.S. Visited Bde HQ 95.	
	19.8.16	—	Sectional duties evacuated my units	
	20.8.16	—	Sectional duties visited my units	
	21.8.16	—	A.D.V.S called in the afternoon to examine the sick sectional duties in the morning	
			Issued Bde HQ 95 sick	
	22.8.16	—	Evacuated 11 sick horses and three mange cases to No 13 Vety Hospital	
	23.9.16	—	Sectional duties examined Bde HQ 95 eighteen	
	24.8.16	—	Sectional duties, examined 1 flow Field Ambulance. A.D.V.S called in	

WAR DIARY
INTELLIGENCE SUMMARY

Army Form C. 2118.

14th Mobile Veterinary Section

Sheet 1/6
August 1916

Place	Date	Hour	Summary of Events and Information	Remarks and references to Appendices
	24.8.16		An afternoon with reference to others under the walker test	
HUCQUELIERS	25.8.16 do		Sectional duties	
	26.8.16		Sectional duties	
	27.8.16		Sectional duties	
	28.8.16		A.D.V.S called to see the sick sectional duties	
	29.8.16		Evacuated two skin cases to No 13 Vety Hospital	
	30.8.16		Sectional duties re mounted Bradt O.L.	
	31.8.16		Sectional duties, rendered say units	
			Nothing closed for the month	

G. I. Harding
Captain A.V.C.
O.C. 14th M.V.S.

WAR DIARY or INTELLIGENCE SUMMARY

11th Mobile Veterinary Section

Sheet 77
September 1916
Army Form C. 2118

Vol 19

Place	Date	Hour	Summary of Events and Information	Remarks and references to Appendices
HUCQUELIERS	1.9.16		Sectional duties, attended the sale of Bde Hd Qts & 7 KCFA.	
	2.9.16		Sectional duties	
	3.9.16		Sectional duties	
	4.9.16		A.D.V.S. visited the section sectional duties	
	5.9.16		Evacuated 1 suspicious skin case, & 7 sick horses to No 13 Vety Hospital NEUFCHATEL	
	6.9.16		Inspected Hk Can Bde Hd Qts, sectional duties	
	7.9.16		Sectional duties attended Bde Hd Qts, A.D.V.S & D.D.V.S inspected the section	
	8.9.16		Evacuated 3 cast cases & 2 vety cases to No 13 Mobile Veterinary Section	
	9.9.16		The section packed up in order of readiness for the move the next day	
	10.9.16		Evacuated 9 remount cases to Hd Qts Mob Hospital NEUFCHATEL. Moved from HUCQUELIERS to MAINTENAY staff Capt 1st Can Bde at HUCQUELIERS left endeavouring staff Capt 1st Can Bde at HUCQUELIERS	
MAINTENAY	11.9.16		the section at 1.30 pm. A echelon started Behilen at 7.20 am arrived 4pm. Moved from MAINTENAY to BRAILLY started Behilen one C.S. waggon endone from Buchner Bde	
BRAILLY	12.9.16		Moved from BRAILLY to YZEUX started Behilen at 7.20 am. A echelon q wan arrived 3.50 pm left one horse behind at BRAILLY, that night section bivouacked	

1st R Noble Veterinary Section

WAR DIARY
or
INTELLIGENCE SUMMARY

Sheet 76
September 1916
Army Form C. 2118

Place	Date	Hour	Summary of Events and Information	Remarks and references to Appendices
VIEUX	13.9.16		Sectional duties remained the same for the day.	
	14.9.16		Moved to BOUSY LES DAOURS started at 6.45 am arrived at 4 pm.	
	15.9.16		The sectional moved to LA NEUVILLE, 3 section 13. 14. 20 mule drawn involved	
LA NEUVILLE	16.9.16		Remained LA NEUVILLE, sent up cut horses to No 20 M.V.S.	
	17.9.16		Moved at 7.30 am to horse was on a field between DAOURS and Pt NOYELLE. arrived at 9.0 am.	
Between JADY RS Pt NOYELLES	18.9.16		Evacuated 12 sick horses to hoy VETY HOSPITAL sectional duties	
	19.9.16		5 cast horses were sent to the 20 H.V.S. from the 1st & 5th sectional duties	
	20.9.16		Sectional duties one private joined the section 92916 F DEELEY from No 12 Vety Hospital	
	21.9.16		Sectional duties evacuated whose to 20 M.V.S.	
	22.9.16		Moved from horse walking area at 10.15 arrived CONDE at 6 pm	
	23.9.16		Moved from CONDE arrived BOURBERS sur CANCHE at six o'clock bivouacked for the night	
	24.9.16		Moved from BOURBERS sur CANCHE started at 10.10 arrived at HIX en ISSART at 4 pm, the horses were hired in the farm	

14th Mobile Veterinary Section

WAR DIARY or **INTELLIGENCE SUMMARY**
(Erase heading not required.)

Army Form C. 2118

Sheet No. 9
September 1916

Place	Date	Hour	Summary of Events and Information	Remarks and references to Appendices
AIRE & ISSART	25.9.16		Sectional duties, visited Bde HQ & sick	
	26.9.16		Moved from AIRE & ISSART to FRESSIN arrived about 11:15, I put the section horses in the coach.	
FRESSIN	27.9.16		Paid men, drew 1200 francs from Paymaster 3rd Cav Div, visited the sick & the brigade.	
	28.9.16		Evacuated 2 sick horses to No 3 Veterinary Hospital, sectional duties	
	29.9.16		Sectional duties, visited the A.D.V.S. in the afternoon	
	30.9.16		Sectional duties, the horses reported for duty, examined the ruling of Bde Hd Qrs & 7 C.F.A.	

Diary closed for the month

G.L. Harding
Capt. A.V.C.
O.C. 14th M.V.S.

A.D.M.S. Motor Ambulance Section
Sheet No. 0
October 1916
Army Form C. 2118.

WAR DIARY or INTELLIGENCE SUMMARY

Place	Date	Hour	Summary of Events and Information	Remarks and references to Appendices
FRESSIN	1.X.16		Examined 1st Cav Field Ambulance, visited sick of the headquarters sectional duties	
"	2.X.16		Examined brigade head quarters, visited the sick. Pte 3753 Ball A.V.C reported for duty	
"	3.X.16		Evacuated 12 sick/lame to No 13 baby Hospital A.D.V.S 3 Cav Div examined lines at HESDIN.	12
"	4.X.16		Sectional duties, examined the sick of brigade headquarters.	
"	5.X.16		Sectional duties, examined the sick of brigade headquarters.	
"	6.X.16		Sectional duties, examined the sick of brigade headquarters & the Cav Field Ambulance.	
"	7.X.16		Sectional duties	
"	8.X.16		Sectional duties	
"	9.X.16		A.D.V.S. called to visit the sick in this section, examined horses of brigade headquarters & their sick	
"	10.X.16		Evacuated 6 sick horses to No 13 Vety Hospital NEUFCHATEL brigade headquarters & the F.A.	6
"	11.X.16		Sectional duties, visited sick of brigade headquarters & of the F.A.	

11th Mobile Veterinary Section

WAR DIARY
or
INTELLIGENCE SUMMARY.

Army Form C. 2118.
Sheet 61
October 9/16
Vol 20

Place	Date	Hour	Summary of Events and Information	Remarks and references to Appendices
PRESSIN	12.x.16		Section transport was inspected by the D.A.D of S. & T.	
"	13.x.16		Sectional duties	
"	14.x.16		Sectional duties	
"	15.x.16		Sectional duties	
"	16.x.16		Inspected brigade headquarters sectional duties, ADVS walked back	
"	17.x.16		Evacuated sick cases sick to No 13 Vety Hospital	
"	18.x.16		Sectional duties visited works headquarters headquarters of the F.A.	
"	19.x.16		Sectional duties visited the sub of brigade headquarters of the F.A.	
"	20.x.16		Section moved from PRESSIN to PLANQUES found good billets for men & horses	
PLANQUES	21.x.16		Visited Hunctarchen Yeomanry saw mules for evacuation	
"	22.x.16		Visited Hunctarchen Yeomanry, declared debility cases for evacuation sectional duties	3
"	23.x.16		Sectional duties ADVS called to visit Ourish Sgt 329 Vacey E.C. A.V.C. reported for duty & sectional duties	
"	24.x.16		Evacuated ??? & 10 sick horses to No 13 Vety Hospital NEUF CHAPEL 2.10	

1/K Mobile Veterinary Section

Sheet 57 Army Form C. 2118.

October 1916

WAR DIARY
or
INTELLIGENCE SUMMARY
(Erase heading not required)

Place	Date	Hour	Summary of Events and Information	Remarks and references to Appendices
PLANQUES	26.x.16		Sectional duties, A.D.V.S. 30th Cav Div & D.D.V.S. Cav Corps inspected the section	
"	27.x.16		Sectional duties, visited the sick of the hundredth Yeomanry	
"	28.x.16		Sectional duties	
"	29.x.16		Visited A.D.V.S. 3 Cav Div at WAILLY, sectional duties	
"	30.x.16		Sectional duties. Visited hundredth Yeomanry to arrange A.D.V.S. 3rd Cav Div called to see the sick.	
"	31.x.16		Evacuated mange case number 5 to 10Y.B. Mobile Veterinary Section at LUCE, the Sick horses evacuated at 13 M.V.S. for the night & returned next day	1, 1.

Arrangements for the month

G. L. Harding Capt A.V.C.
O.C. 1st Mobile Veterinary Section

N.K. Mobilisation of Section.

WAR DIARY Sheet 83.
or
INTELLIGENCE SUMMARY. Nov 1916

Army Form C. 2118.

Vol 21

Place	Date	Hour	Summary of Events and Information	Remarks and references to Appendices
PLANQUES	1.11.16	—	Sectional duties	
	2.11.16		Visited hutments Germany. Saw the sick. Sectional duties.	
	3.11.16	—	Sectional duties.	
	4.11.16		Sectional duties, visited the hutments Germany.	
	5.11.16		Sectional duties.	
	6.11.16		Sectional duties. A.D.V.S. called to see the sick	
	7.11.16		Sectional duties visited the hutments Germany	
	8.11.16		Sectional duties.	
	9.11.16		Inspected hutments Germany with A.D.V.S. all horses.	
	10.11.16		Sectional duties.	
	11.11.16		Visited hutments Germany sectional duties.	
	12.11.16		Visited hutments Germany evacuated 2 No Mobilektrumay section sick returned cosvalus	
			A.D.V.S called to visit the sick	
	13.11.16		Evacuated 2 mange cases and another horse to 20 M.V.S, the	
	14.11.16		sent via 13 M.V.S & 13 Vety Hospital	

14K Mobile Veterinary Section Sheet 54. Army Form C. 2118.

WAR DIARY
or INTELLIGENCE SUMMARY.

No. vqu6

Place	Date	Hour	Summary of Events and Information	Remarks and references to Appendices
PLANQUES	15.11.16		Visited Horselines framing to see remount escutcheon.	
	16.11.16		Sectional duties.	
	17.11.16		Visited horselines. Yoken army on the sick.	
	18.11.16		Sectional duties.	
	19.11.16		Sectional duties.	
	20.11.16		Sectional duties. A.D.V.S. called to see the sick.	
	21.11.16		Sectional duties. Visited horselines. Yoken army.	
	22.11.16		Evacuated two mange cases and one cut Mare to the 13.M. Mob Vet Sect. Sent on to the 13 Vety Hospital.	
	23.11.16		A.D.V.S. and D.D.V.S. Corps inspected & sectional duties.	
	24.11.16			
	25.11.16		Proceeded on leave to England (authority A.D.V.S. 30th div) Took over duties from Capt Hardy, who visited by A.D.V.S. 3rd Can Div	
	26.11.16		Also inspected Lines	
	27.11.16		Sectional duties	
	28.11.16		Visited Dublin. Evacuated 2 horses to 13 M.V.S.	

11th Mobile Veterinary Section.

WAR DIARY or INTELLIGENCE SUMMARY.

Sheet 45.
Nov 1916

Army Form C. 2118.

(Erase heading not required.)

Place	Date	Hour	Summary of Events and Information	Remarks and references to Appendices
PLANQUES	23/11/16		Admitted Rabies	
"	29/11/16		Admitted Rabies, on Horse 4 Gov.t Remount Depot 1 Field Ambulance	
"	1/12/16		Admitted	

Diary closed for the Month of November 1916

J S Hopkins
Capt A.V.C.

WAR DIARY or INTELLIGENCE SUMMARY

Army Form C. 2118.

11th Mobile Veterinary Section

Sheet 86   W MVS   Vol 2

Place	Date	Hour	Summary of Events and Information	Remarks and references to Appendices
PLANQUES	1/12/16		Medical duties. Inspected by Brig Gen Pickett 17 Cav Bde.	
"	2/12/16		Medical duties.	
"	3/12/16		Medical duties.	
"	4/12/16		Medical duties, admitted 4 sick horse evacuated 3 AOW	
			3rd Can Bde Vet reported sick.	
			Medical duties assisted to sick horses to 13 M.V.S.	
	5/12/16		Medical duties evacuated 5 sick horses to 13 M.V.S.	
	6.12.16		Returned from leave, I took charge of section from Capt Hodd A.V.C.	
	7.12.16		Visited Lancasterhin Yeomanry, sectional duties.	
	8.12.16		Sectional duties.	
	9.12.16		Visited Lancastershin Yeomanry & H Coy Bde Head quarters.	
	10.12.16		Visited Lancasterhin Yeomanry & K Bty R H A.	
	11.12.16		Visited Bde H Qts, sectional duties.	
	12.12.16		Visited Lancasterhin Yeomanry & 1st H to Guerver	
	13.12.16		Evacuated 1 sick horse to No 18 Veterinary Section by road	
			Visited Bde HdQts.	
	14.12.16		Visited Bde Hd Qts, 61st Lifeguards.	

WAR DIARY or INTELLIGENCE SUMMARY

Army Form C. 2118.

2nd Mobile Veterinary Section. Sheet 67.

Place	Date	Hour	Summary of Events and Information	Remarks and references to Appendices
PLANQUES	15.12.16		Noted horses of Yeomanry & RHA R.H.A. Kept in two veterinary cases from flu.	
	16.12.16		Visited B.de H.d Q.Rs. & 1st Life Guards.	
	17.12.16		Inspected B squadron Leicestershire Yeomanry.	
	18.12.16		Attended quarterly remount cases at TORCY & FRUGES FRESSIN. A.D.V.S. & D.D.R. were present.	
	19.12.16		Visited Bde Hd Qrs evacuated 15 sick horses & 1 manage & 1 suspicious.	15, 1, 1.
			mange case at HESDIN.	
	20.12.16		Visited Bde Hd Qrs sectional duties.	
	21.12.16		Visited the Leicestershire Yeomanry sectional duties.	
	22.12.16		Sectional duties, visited Bde Hd Qrs sec.	
	23.12.16		Sectional duties, visited the Leicestershire Yeomanry.	
	24.12.16		Sectional duties, visited Leicestershire Yeomanry.	
	25.12.16		Sectional duties	
	26.12.16		Took in 26 remount cases, cast by D.D.R, 3 were returned to the 3rd Life Guards, faulty description one remount case was made a veterinary case.	26, 3 1

WAR DIARY or INTELLIGENCE SUMMARY

11th Mobile Veterinary Section.

Army Form C. 2118.

Sheet 46.

Place	Date	Hour	Summary of Events and Information	Remarks and references to Appendices
PLANQUES	26.12.16		Visited 2nd life Guards to see sick, sectional duties.	
"	27		Evacuated 22 remount case, 2 mange cases, & 1 oedema to Nº 18 Vety Hosp	X9, 2, 1
"	28.12.16		visited Lauchachie Yeomanry.	
"	29.12.16		Visited 2nd life Guards & Lincolnshire Yeomanry, sectional duties	
"	30.12.16		Sectional duties, visited 1st Lincolnshire Yeomanry	
"	31.12.16		Sectional duties	

Diary closed for the month

G. C. Hardy
Capt. A.V.C.
O.C. 11th M.V.S.

1/1 K Mobile Veterinary Section — **January 1917** — **Sheet 59.**

WAR DIARY or INTELLIGENCE SUMMARY
Army Form C. 2118.

Vol 23

Place	Date	Hour	Summary of Events and Information	Remarks and references to Appendices
PLANQUES	1.1.17	—	Sectional duties, visited Leicestershire Yeomanry head quarters & to squadron.	
	2.1.17		Sectional duties.	
	3.1.17		Sectional duties, visited Leicestershire Yeomanry.	
	4.1.17		Sectional duties, A.D.V.S. called to see the sick.	
	5.1.17		Evacuated 3 mange cases, 3 ulcerative cases, to sick horses at HATFSQUEL	2, 3, 5.
	6.1.17		Visited Leicestershire Yeomanry, examined Brigadier, made arrangements for the prevention of the spread of mange in the squadron.	
	7.1.17		Sectional duties, examined the Aux Horse Transport horses.	1, 6.
	8.1.17		Sectional duties, visited Brigadier Leicestershire Yeomanry, Post Mor. 1 Cpl. & found to die-month (the premises & dogs the imitant mange cases.	
	9.1.17		Sectional duties, visited the Leicestershire Yeomanry.	
	10.1.17		Sectional duties, sent 1 Cpl. & Groom to dress Ulcerative mange cases at the Leicestershire Yeomanry.	

14th Mobile Veterinary Section

WAR DIARY
or
INTELLIGENCE SUMMARY.
(Erase heading not required.)

Army Form C. 2118.

January 1917   Sheet 90.

Place	Date	Hour	Summary of Events and Information	Remarks and references to Appendices
PLANQUES	11.1.17		A.D.V.S. called to see sick sectional duties.	
	12.1.17		Sectional duties.	
	13.1.17		Evacuated 4 sick horse & mange case to No 13 Veterinary Hospital.	Ht. 1.
			Inspected Lancashire Hussars Yeomanry.	
			Sectional duties.	
	14.1.17		Inspected A squadron Lancashire Hussars Yeomanry & squadron in the afternoon saw sick tent horses.	
	15.1.17			
	16.1.17		Sent over a Cpl to Lancashire Yeomanry to superintend the dressing of two mentaut mange cases & sectional duties.	
			Inspected C squadron Lancashire Hussars Yeomanry sectional duties.	
	17.1.17		Sectional duties, A.D.V.S. called to visit the sick.	
	18.1.17		Evacuated 15 sick horses and 1 mange case to No 13 Veterinary Hospital.	S, 1.
	19.1.17		Examined B squadron Lancashire Yeomanry and regimental.	
	20.1.17		Sectional duties.	
	21.1.17		Sectional duties.	
	22.1.17		Examined A squadron Lancashire Hussars Yeomanry & regimental.	

WAR DIARY or INTELLIGENCE SUMMARY

17th Mobile Veterinary Section   January 1917   Sheet 91.

Army Form C. 2118.

Place	Date	Hour	Summary of Events and Information	Remarks and references to Appendices
PLANQUES	23.1.17		Sectional duties.	
	24.1.17		Examined Cagnadien heuse the one Yeomanry, 3 sent at headquarters, sectional duties.	
	25.1.17		A.D.V.S. called to see the sick for evacuation, sectional duties.	
	26.1.17		Evacuated 3 sick horses to No 10 Veterinary Hospital. G.O.C. commanding the brigade inspected the section.	
	27.1.17		Sectional duties.	
	28.1.17		Sectional duties. Inocated the horses of the Yeomanry.	
	29.1.17		Sectional duties.	
	30.1.17		Sectional duties.	
	31.1.17		Sectional duties.	

Diary closed for the month.

E. E. Harding
Capt. A.V.C.
O.C. 17th M.V.S.

WAR DIARY or INTELLIGENCE SUMMARY

Army Form C. 2118.

D.A.D. Mobile Veterinary Section
February 1917
Sheet 92
Vol 2

Place	Date	Hour	Summary of Events and Information	Remarks and references to Appendices
CUCQ	1.2.17		Section moved from PLANQUES KLUCQ, passed HADDON 2 p.m. & BADDEN 4 p.m. Sent on foot our billets & bivouacs, were inspected by the 20 M.V.S.	
	2.2.17		Sectional duties. Visited hacketerie farriery & divisional school	
	3.2.17		Sectional duties	
	4.2.17		Sectional duties, visited hacketerie farriery divisional school	
	5.2.17		Sectional duties	
	6.2.17		Sectional duties, visited hacketerie farriery	
	7.2.17		Sectional duties, visited hacketerie farriery, divisional school	
	8.2.17		Section at duties, visited veterinary lines	
	9.2.17		Visited hacketerie farriery divisional school. A.D.V.S. called	
	10.2.17		Examined supply hacketerie farriery, visited the sick cases & convalescent lines	
	11.2.17		Sectional duties	
	12.2.17		Sectional duties, examined & supply of hacketerie farriery and sick of the regiment	
	13.2.17		Sectional duties, visited veterinary charges	

WAR DIARY or INTELLIGENCE SUMMARY

Army Form C. 2118.

14th Mobile Veterinary Section

February 1917 Sheet 93

Place	Date	Hour	Summary of Events and Information	Remarks and references to Appendices
CuCQ	14.2.17		Sectional duties attended veterinary charger.	
	15.2.17		Sectional duties, attended veterinary charger. Football match vs M.P.M. Cav. Corps.	
	16.2.17		Sectional duties	
	17.2.17		Visited veterinary charger. Sectional duties	
	18.2.17		Sectional duties	
	19.2.17		Sectional duties. Visited Huestache Yvannay & unusual value.	
	20.2.17		Sectional duties. Visited veterinary charger.	
	21.2.17		Sectional duties ransacking Lucestache Yvannay	
	22.2.17		Visited Huestache Yvannay & unusual value.	
	23.2.17		Visited Huestache Yvannay. Sectional duties.	
	24.2.17		Went with A.D.V.S. to ENOCQ to see new method of securing hues cauredart, visited Huestache Yvannay & unusual value	
	25.2.17		Sectional duties visited Huestache Yvannay & unusual value	
			Sto Att f good reported to duty from No 10 Vy Hospital.	
	26.2.17		Sectional duties visited Huestache Yvannay & Im whole	
	27.2.17		Sectional duties A.D.V.S. called whole morning, visited Huestache Yvannay	

WAR DIARY
or
INTELLIGENCE SUMMARY

Army Form C. 2118.

February 1917 Sheet 7A

(Erase heading not required.)

Place	Date	Hour	Summary of Events and Information	Remarks and references to Appendices
LVC Q	26/2/17		Cut and destroyed unmarked shrubs from any attacked sect. 3 V 5 in the afternoon. Nothing else on for the month. G. E. Harding Capt. ANC.	

Army Form C. 2118.

1/1 K Middlesex Yeomany Sectn

WAR DIARY
or
INTELLIGENCE SUMMARY.
(Erase heading not required.)

March 1917 Sheet 96   Vol 25

Instructions regarding War Diaries and Intelligence Summaries are contained in F. S. Regs., Part II. and the Staff Manual respectively. Title pages will be prepared in manuscript.

Place	Date	Hour	Summary of Events and Information	Remarks and references to Appendices
Cul Q	1.3.17		Visited Leicestershire Yeomanry, sect med duties, called in the afternoon	3, 2
	2.3.17		Evacuated 3 sick hurses to No 13 lkly Hospital. 2 hurses were sent turfram	
	3.3.17		No 20 Mobile Vety Sect' now being evacuated by road. Visited Leicestershire Yeomanry consist of 7 Squadron. The Others were sent to No 9 Vety Hospital, sect med duties	
	4.3.17		Visited Leicestershire Yeomanry to see to sick	
	5.3.17		Visited Leicestershire Yeomanry, sect med duties	
	6.3.17		Visited Leicestershire Yeomanry A.D.V.S called in the afternoon	
	7.3.17		Visited Leicestershire Yeomanry, sect med duties	
	8.3.17		Went with A.D.V.S. to see recty Cases of Leicestershire Yeomanry, visited divisional school milk the A.D.V.S	
	9.3.17		Sect med duties. A.D.V.S. called in the afternoon	
	10.3.17		Visited Leicestershire Yeomanry	
	11.3.17		Sect med duties	
	12.3.17		Visited Leicestershire Yeomanry, sect med duties	
	13.3.17		Sect med duties	

Army Form C. 2118.

WAR DIARY
or
INTELLIGENCE SUMMARY.
(Erase heading not required.)

14th Mobile Veterinary Section
March 1917
Sheet of

Instructions regarding War Diaries and Intelligence Summaries are contained in F. S. Regs., Part II. and the Staff Manual respectively. Title pages will be prepared in manuscript.

Place	Date	Hour	Summary of Events and Information	Remarks and references to Appendices
Cul Q	14.3.17		Visited horse lines forenoon, sectional duties	
	15.3.17		Sectional duties, went to Mob Vety Section to see horses, horse lines in forenoon, drifted, this was cancelled.	
	16.3.17		Sectional duties, visited horse lines forenoon	
	17.3.17		Sectional duties, A.D.V.S. called in the afternoon	
	18.3.17		Sectional duties	
	19.3.17		Visited horse lines forenoon, took in 20 sick horses, A.D.V.S. called in the afternoon to see animals	
	20.3.17		Visited horse lines forenoon & I went to school, evacuated 20 sick horses and 1 mange case to M.D.13 Vety Hospital	
	21.3.17		Sectional duties, I took in 15 sick horses from the Car Base A.D.V.S. evacuated them in the afternoon	
	22.3.17		Sectional duties visited horselines forenoon in the morning went out A.D.V.S. to 20 M.V.S. to arrange about receiving 31 horses from 6th Cav Bde 31. evacuated 9 sick horses dift mange cases to Mob Vety Sectional Vety Hospital	
	23.3.17		Sectional duties, received 31 horses from 6th Mob Vety Sectional	
	24.3.17		evacuated 30 horses from 6th Cav Bde, sectional duties	

WAR DIARY or INTELLIGENCE SUMMARY

Army Form C. 2118.

March 1917 Shall 90th

Place	Date	Hour	Summary of Events and Information	Remarks and references to Appendices
C.u.C. Q	25.3.17		Sectional duties marked Inspection. Sgt H/g Elwick F reported for duty.	
	27.3.17		Sectional duties marked Inspection of wounds. Staff Sgt Vasey E.G. was sent to No 6 Vety Hospital.	
	28.3.17		Sgt Irgant duties, marked F.S.V.S.	
	29.3.17		Evacuated 10 horses from 2 M.V.S. & 3 remount cases.	
	30.3.17		Sectional duties. Inspected cat. mr. for a bye-gate marking order next day. Addition of set van under the brigade, in Rung du FLIERS.	
	31.3.17		CAMPIENEUILLES & TRANDES ST Aubin diet until 12.15 pm. Inspected horse-standings. Yammery horses fr. cutting by remount officer. Set shade duties.	

Diary closed for the month
E. Harding
Capt. a.D.C

WAR DIARY
INTELLIGENCE SUMMARY

Lt K Noble Veterinary Sn'en. April 1917 Sheet 9 &. Army Form C. 2118.

Vol 26

Place	Date	Hour	Summary of Events and Information	Remarks and references to Appendices
LUCQ	1.4.17		Sat. rout. duties, visited A.D.V.S.	
	2.4.17		Sat. rout. duties, attended a sitting parade of remounts by D.J.R. visited horse tache harness	
	3.4.17		Sat. rout. duties	
	4.4.17		Sat. rout. duties, evacuated 2 horses & 2 from 21 Mobile Vet. Sn.	22, 3.
	5.4.17		Moved from LUCQ to BEAUVRAINVILLE	
BEAUVRAIN-VILLE	6.4.17		Evacuated 11 mules & 2 sick horses to No 13 Vety Hospital. 603 acting paid Sergt Lawrence R was deprived of his act of rank.	
	7.4.17		Moved from BEAUVRAINVILLE to BOURBERS sur CANCHE	
	8.4.17		Sections of division were demobilised and allocated to GOUY EN ARTOIS.	
	9.4.17		Moved from GOUY ARTOIS to x roads 2 miles W of ARRAS	
Roads	10.4.17		Stood to	
	11.4.17		"	
	12.4.17		Evacuated 32 horses as nulls to No 22 Vety Hospital from AGNES LES DUISANS	23, 3.
	13.4.17		Evacuated 32 horses to No 22 Vety Hospital from AGNES LES DUISANS	
	14.4.17		Sat. rout. duties	

14th Mobile Veterinary Section.

WAR DIARY or INTELLIGENCE SUMMARY.

April 1917 — sheet 99

Army Form C. 2118.

Place	Date	Hour	Summary of Events and Information	Remarks and references to Appendices
X Roads 3 kms W/FARAS	15.4.17		Evacuated positions at GENESLES JUISANS, section moved to BERNEVILLE	
	16.4.17		Moved from BERNEVILLE to FROHEN LE GRAND, gibs Spr Smet, Spr Tharyce w/y	
FROHEN LE GRAND	17.4.17		Sectional duties, visited horse lines of various g.o.many. Pte 60 Laurence T. Evacuated to No 3 Veterinary hospital	
	18.4.17		Sectional duties Spr 191 Walls [?]. It evacuated 1st 4 to Multonbun Cavalry (CS) wounded 2.5 horses at	
	19.4.17		Section moved from FROHEN LE GRAND to TORTEFONTAINE, wanted 2 hrs at BOUQUEMAISON, collected 1 mule from BEAUVOIR RIVIERE	
TORTEFONT-AINE	20.4.17		Sectional duties.	
	21.4.17		Sectional duties, visited Bde headquarters & 9th Cavalry field Ambulance.	
	22.4.17		Sectional duties, 1 J.N.S called in T.......y	
	23.4.17		Sectional duties, visited Bgd headquarters & of Cavalry field Ambulance.	
	24.4.17		Evacuated Horsham 61 mule to hospitality hospital, entrained at BEAUVRAINEVILLE. Went 2 LS Thompson from 20 Middlesex sick to hospital sickness.	
	25.4.17		Rode up the & 1 man to veteran sub horses left on line, 7 mule villated. Entrans of 2nd life Guards from BEALCOURT	
	26.4.17		Sectional duties, visited Bgd headquarters & of Cavalry field Ambulance.	

2353 Wt. W2544/1454 700,000 5/15 D. D. & L. A.D.S.S./Forms/C. 2118.

WAR DIARY
or
INTELLIGENCE SUMMARY.

Army Form C. 2118.

Sheet No. 00

April, 1917

Place	Date	Hour	Summary of Events and Information	Remarks and references to Appendices
TORTEFONT-AINE	28.4.17		Sent Pack to LILLERS L'HOPITAL to collect one tent lot by 2nd Rep Garden. Several duties.	
	29.4.17		Sectional duties & SBN's collected	
	30.4.17		Evacuated to Home and sends from BEAURAINEVILLE to Army Rest Hospital. One period of 10 Cavalry Field Ambulance, visited recedence of Brigade Headquarter	

Busy Areas for the month

G. E. Harding
Capt. R.A.M.C.

1/1 K. Noble Veterinary Section

14th Mob. Vety Section
Sheet 101
Army Form C.2118.

Aug. 1917

Vol 27

WAR DIARY or INTELLIGENCE SUMMARY

(Erase heading not required.)

Place	Date	Hour	Summary of Events and Information	Remarks and references to Appendices
TORTEFONTAINE	1.8.17		Sectional duties visited brigade headquarters	
"	2.8.17		Sectional duties. The transport of the Section was inspected by the O.C A.S.C.	
"	3.8.17		Sular. As this was now very full, 6 draught mules, 1 G.S. wagon & 4 S. mules	
"	4.8.17		Sectional duties, visited brigade headquarters and of Cavalry field Ambulance	
"	5.8.17		Sectional duties, visited brigade headquarters and of Cavalry field Ambulance	
"	6.8.17		Sectional duties	
"	7.8.17		Sectional duties	
"	8.8.17		Sectional duties	
"	9.8.17		Sectional duties, visited of Cavalry field Ambulance and brigade headquarters	13, 8, 3, 19
"	10.8.17		Sectional duties, visited of Cavalry field Ambulance and brigade headquarters	
			Evacuated to 3 horses and 6 mules (32 remount camp 19 My canny) to N.013	
			Vety Hospital at NEUFCHATEL from the nullah at BEAURAINVILLE.	
"	11.8.17		Sectional duties	
"	12.8.17		Section moved from TORTEFONTAINE to VULX and billeted there for the night.	
	13.8.17		Section moved to GEZAINCOURT, horses were in a field, men had a tarpaulin.	

1st Northumberland? ??

WAR DIARY
or
INTELLIGENCE SUMMARY.
(Erase heading not required.)

Army Form C. 2118.

Sheet No ?

May 1919

Place	Date	Hour	Summary of Events and Information	Remarks and references to Appendices
Marquay	14/5/19		Section moved to VILLERS BOCAGE, horses were put in a field, all men were under cover.	
	15/5/19		Section moved from VILLERS BOCAGE to FOUILLOY, all horses were put under cover, the men bivouaced.	
FOUILLOY	16/5/19		Section remained here for the day. Sh. 7k 0 & 27 59 Jeanne d'Arc TK 239799	
	17/5/19		Section reported for duty to Corps Cavalry, established Sections moved to CERISY, men ad horses bivouaced. The horses were all put under cover.	
CERISY	18/5/19		Section duties worked brigade hq and water duty of Corps Cavalry	
	19/5/19		Section moved from CERISY to a point N.E. of BUIRE (Map ref. J 25)	
Nr J BUIRE	20/5/19		Section duties, watered my unit, horses were fed with German biscuit.	
	21/5/19		Section duties, watered my unit	
	22/5/19		The unity attended the boot baths in passing times. Evacuated 3 sewage cases and sent there to hosp Nery Hospital FORGES LES EAUX from here killed 6	
	23/5/19		LA CAPELLETTE Sectional duties worked my unit	

2353 Wt. W2544/1454 700,000 5/15 D.D.&L. A.D.S.S./Forms/C. 2118.

WAR DIARY
of
INTELLIGENCE SUMMARY.
(Erase heading not required.)

Sheet 103
Army Form C. 2118.

May 1917

Place	Date	Hour	Summary of Events and Information	Remarks and references to Appendices
W. of BUIRE	24/5/17		Sectional duties. Visited advanced Divn Headquarters (advanced) to inspect kitchens.	
	25/5/17		Visited Brigade Headquarters and 1/Cav Fd Ambulance.	
	26/5/17		Sectional duties. Visited Divisional Headquarters at VILLERS FAUCON	
	27/5/17		Sectional duties. Visited 2nd Cav Fd Ambulance and Brigade Headquarters.	
	28/5/17		Sectional duties.	
	29/5/17		Sectional duties. Visited Brigade Headquarters & 1st Cavalry Field Ambulance.	
	30/5/17		Sectional duties. Visited Divisional Headquarters.	
	31/5/17		Sectional duties.	
			Sectional duties. Visited Brigade Headquarters & 1st Cavalry Fd Ambulance.	
			Diary closed for the month.	
			E. E. Macdonald Capt. R.A.M.C.	

WAR DIARY / INTELLIGENCE SUMMARY

Army Form C. 2118.

Sheet 10th — 1st Mobile Veterinary Section

June 1917

Place	Date	Hour	Summary of Events and Information	Remarks and references to Appendices
Sheet 62 D.20. NE of BUIRE	1.6.17		Sectional duties, worked my veterinary charges	
	2.6.17		Evacuated 15 sick horses, mange cases & while mange, from TINCOURT station to No 1 Vety Hospital. Cart horse was provided with 2 two gallon filters tins of water for the journey.	15, 1, 1. 2. 1.
	3.6.17		Routine duties, visited my units	
	4.6.17		Sectional duties visited all V.O.s held by 4 D.V.S at FLAMICOURT in the afternoon	
	5.6.17		Sectional duties, awarded 7.28.g.199 Pte Dean H. A.V.C. 10 days trial punishment No 1 in Ho following charge "Not complying with an order "Infact" reply to an N.C.O. Pte 38653 Ball, J.F.A.V.C. was sent to O.B.y. Southern temporarily transferred to N.F.P	
	6.6.17		Routine duties, visited my veterinary charges	
	7.6.17		Routine duties	
	8.6.17		Routine duties	
	9.6.17		Routine duties	
	10.6.17		Routine duties	
	11.6.17		Routine duties, A.D.V.S inspected horses for evacuation	

Sheet 105

1st K. Mobile Veterinary Sec'n   Army Form C. 2118.

WAR DIARY
or
INTELLIGENCE SUMMARY.
(Erase heading not required.)

June 1917

Place	Date	Hour	Summary of Events and Information	Remarks and references to Appendices
Sheet 62c Y.22. N.E. of BUIRE	12.6.17		Evacuated 5 sick horses @ 2 mules to No. 7 Vety Hospital, and enclosed 7 to 20. M.V.S.	5, 7, 1.
	13.6.17		Routine duties	
	14.6.17		Attended a course of gas instruction at the Divisional Gas School at LONGAVESNES, in accordance with orders received from the A.D.V.S. 3rd Can. Div.	
	15.6.17		Routine duties. Attended Gas School	
	16.6.17		Routine duties, attended Gas School. Sgt 9166 Stone, P. attended the above course and passed.	
	17.6.17		Went to LONGAVESNES to see horse sent through the gas with the new respirator. He appeared very successful. All horses were not inconvenienced	S. 1.
	18.6.17		Routine duties.	
	19.6.17		Evacuated 6 sick horses, and 1 mange case to No. 7 Vety Hospital	
	20.6.17		Routine duties.	
	21.6.17		Routine duties	
	22.6.17		Routine duties. Pte Hobbs A.J. A.V.C. 17/7/17 refused for duty from No. 7 Vety Hospital	
	23.6.17		Routine duties	
	24.6.17		Routine duties. Inspected my units.	

Sheet 10 of.

WAR DIARY 14th Mobile Veterinary Section. Army Form C. 2118.
or
INTELLIGENCE SUMMARY. June 1917.

(Erase heading not required.)

Place	Date	Hour	Summary of Events and Information	Remarks and references to Appendices
Near 62.C.2.22. NE of BUIRE	25.6.17		Routine duties	
	26.6.17		Evacuated 27 horses from TINCOURT to No 7 Vety Hospital, routine duties	4.
	27.6.17		Routine duties	
	28.6.17		Routine duties	
	29.6.17		Routine duties, 14 M V S inspected horses for evacuation	
	30.6.17		Evacuated 46 sick horses, mange cases, and one mule to No 7 Vety Hospital.	8.7.1

Strength return for the month

G.E. Harding
Capt A.V.C.
O.C. 14th M.V.S.

Sheet 104

WAR DIARY
or
INTELLIGENCE SUMMARY.
(Erase heading not required.)

11th Mobile Veterinary Section
Army Form C. 2118.
July 1917
Vol 2B

Place	Date	Hour	Summary of Events and Information	Remarks and references to Appendices
NE of BUIRE Sheet 62c Y.23	1.7.17		Sectional duties, visited my units	
	2.7.17		Sectional packed up for the move the following day/sectional duties Evacuated one horse from TINCOURT station, this was taken down by the	
	3.7.17		13 M.V.S. Section moved to SUZANNE area camp 50' and bivouaced 20 M.V.S. sent its horse from SUZANNE to BUIRE area to attach a horse of the Bde Major and it moved that night. Section arrived at SUZANNE at 3 pm	
SUZANNE	4.7.17		Remained here for the day, sectional duties	
	5.7.17		Section moved to HEILLY arrived 12 noon and bivouaced, received one horse from the 1st Life Guards	
	6.7.17		Section moved to ORVILLE and arrived at 3 pm left one horse 1st Life Guards at HEILLY, it was unable to travel	
	7.7.17		Section moved from ORVILLE to RIBEUVILLETTE arrived 12 noon and bivouaced	
	8.7.17		Section moved near village of BERLES and arrived 9.45 am	

Sheet 159

WAR DIARY 11th Mobile Veterinary Section Army Form C. 2118.
or
INTELLIGENCE SUMMARY.   July 9/17

Place	Date	Hour	Summary of Events and Information	Remarks and references to Appendices
BERLES	9.7.17		Sectional duties, visited my units	
"	10.7.17		Sectional duties	
"	11.7.17		Sectional duties	
"	12.7.17		Sectional duties. A.D.V.S. visited the sick horses for evacuation.	
"	13.7.17		Evacuated 5 sick horses, 1 mule, 1 mange case to No 2 Vety Hospital from TINQUES sectional duties	
"	14.7.17		Sectional duties, visited my veterinary chargers	
"	15.7.17		Sectional duties	
"	16.7.17		Section moved to AUCHEL arrived at 11.30 am. Later one horse at BERLES of 7th C.F.A but was moved to the RUE de GUARBECQUE arrived at 9.10 am	
"	17.7.17		Sectional duties	
"	18.7.17		D.J.V.S. Car arrives inspected the section	
"	19.7.17		Sectional duties. Pte 14631 Wilkinson T.B. A.V.C. reported for duty from No 19 Vety Hospital	
"	20.7.17		Evacuated 15 horses from FIRE to 22 Vety Hospital 5 mange 10 sick	15,10.
"	21.7.17			

Sheet 110.

WAR DIARY
or
INTELLIGENCE SUMMARY.

Army Form C. 2118.

14th Mobile Veterinary Section.

July 1917.

Place	Date	Hour	Summary of Events and Information	Remarks and references to Appendices
Rue de GUARBECQUES	22.7.17		Pte 465 Woodyer P.H.V.C was sent to No 9 Vety Hospital	
	23.7.17		Sectional duties	
	24.7.17		Sectional duties, visited my units	
	25.7.17		Sectional duties, visited my units	
	26.7.17		Evacuated 6 sick horses from A.T.R.E to 2.2 Vety Hospital through the 30.M.V.S.	
	27.7.17		Sectional duties, visited my units	
	28.7.17		Sectional duties, visited my units	
	29.7.17		Sectional duties, visited my units	
	30.7.17		Sectional duties, visited my units	
	31.7.17		Evacuated 4 sick horses and 1 mule (2 mange cases) to No 2 Vety Hospital from A.T.R.E. Sectional duties.	

Diary closed for the month.
G L Harding
Capt. A.V.C.

WAR DIARY
INTELLIGENCE SUMMARY

Sheet III

14th Mobile Veterinary Section. August 1917.

Army Form C. 2118

Vol 30

Place	Date	Hour	Summary of Events and Information	Remarks and references to Appendices
RUE de GUARBECQUES	1.8.17		Sectional duties, visited my units	
"	2.8.17		" " " " "	
"	3.8.17		" " " " "	
"	4.8.17		" " " " "	
"	5.8.17		" " " " "	
"	6.8.17		Sectional duties, admitted horses for evacuation	
"	7.8.17		Evacuated 6 horses & 3 mules from N.I.R.E. to No 32 Vety Hospital	6, 3
"	8.8.17		Sectional duties, visited my units	
"	9.8.17		Sectional duties	
"	10/8/17		Sectional duties & visited my units - Took up from office Monday A.V.	
"	11/8/17		do	
"	12/8/17		do	
"	13/8/17		do	
"	14/8/17		do	
"	15/8/17		do	

L.t.H.

Sheet 113

WAR DIARY
or
INTELLIGENCE SUMMARY.
(Erase heading not required.)

14th Mobile Veterinary Section Army Form C. 2118.

August 1917.

Place	Date	Hour	Summary of Events and Information	Remarks and references to Appendices
RUE de GUARBECQUE	16/8/17		Received Mules & evacuated any sick	
	17/8/17		Evacuated 12 horses & 1 mule to No 22 Vety Hospital ABBEVILLE from AIRE on horse & motorbike ambulance	
"	18/8/17		Received Mules & evacuated any sick	
"	19/8/17		" " " "	
"	20/8/17		" " " "	
"	21/8/17		" " " "	
"	22/8/17		" Started with F/Capt G.C. Stanley A.V.C. for the field of operation	
"	23.8.17		Sectional duties	
"	24.8.17		Evacuated 4 sick horse to 22 Vety Hospital from AIRE sectional duties	4.
"	25.8.17		Took over the veterinary charges of Capt J W Heelis A.V.C. 1st Life Guards, 1st Machine Gun Squadron & R Battery R.H.A.	
"	26.8.17		Sectional duties, visited my units	
"	27.8.17		Sectional duties, evacuated one mule sent to the section found by 2nd Cav Div. Reserve Park and sent by D.R. this was sent through the 20 M.V.S. G.L.H.	

Sheet 113.

1st K. Mobile Veterinary Section
August 1917.

Army Form C. 2118.

WAR DIARY
or
INTELLIGENCE SUMMARY.
(Erase heading not required.)

Place	Date	Hour	Summary of Events and Information	Remarks and references to Appendices
RUE DE GUARBECQUE	28-6-17		Sectional duties, Section was inspected by D.D.V.S. en route and A.D.V.S. 2nd Cav. Div.	
"	29-8-17		Sectional duties	
"	30-8-17		Sectional duties	
"	31-8-17		Admitted horses for evacuation, these were inspected by the # D.V.S. Visited my units.	
			Diary closed for the month.	
			G.L. Mawany Capt AVC O.C. 1st M.V.S.	

14th Natal Veterinary Section

WAR DIARY or **INTELLIGENCE SUMMARY**

September 1917
Sheet 1/4

Army Form C. 2118.

Vol 31

Place	Date	Hour	Summary of Events and Information	Remarks and references to Appendices
RUE DE GUARBÉCQUE	1.9.17		Evacuated from sick horse lines to No 2 Vety Hospital from AIRE, section handed for move on the following day.	4
BOURS	2.9.17		Section moved to BOURS (transsheet 1), horse went full under own also Human	
	3.9.17		Sectional duties, worked of Marine Hospital for life guards, Brigade Head Quarters and of Combined Ambulance	
	4.9.17		Sectional duties, visited RSA Army RHA.	
	5.9.17		Visited Lancashire Yeomanry in the morning, A.D.V.S visited the section in the afternoon	
	6.9.17		Sectional duties, horses were inspected by M.O for scabies in afternoon	
	7.9.17		Sectional duties, visited regiments.	
	8.9.17		Sectional duties, visited regiments.	
	9.9.17		Sectional duties, visited regiments.	
	10.9.17		Sectional duties, visited regiments.	
	11.9.17		J.D.V.S Canaby Loops visited A.D.V.S and Lancashire Division inspected the section admitted horses for examination	
	12.9.17		Evacuated eight subjects to No 7 Veterinary Hospital sectional duties.	

L.E.H.

WAR DIARY
or
INTELLIGENCE SUMMARY

(Erase heading not required.)

Army Form C. 2118.

D.A.D.M.S. L of C Area any Salkan

September 1917
Sheet 116.

Place	Date	Hour	Summary of Events and Information	Remarks and references to Appendices
BOURS	13.9.17		Sectional duties visited my unit.	
	14.9.17		Sectional duties visited my unit	
	15.9.17		Sectional duties visited my unit	
	16.9.17		Sectional duties visited my unit	
	17.9.17		Sectional duties visited my unit	
	18.9.17		Transport of the saloon was inspected by the O.C. A.S.C. A.J.V.S. 30 Can Div. examined horses for examination.	
	19.9.17		Evacuated 17 sick horses to No 7 Veterinary Hospital from LILLERS	4.
	20.9.17		Evacuated 39 sick remount cases to No 7 Veterinary Hospital from LILLERS	
	21.9.17		Sectional duties visited my unit.	
	22.9.17		Sectional duties visited my unit	
	23.9.17		Sectional duties visited my unit	
	24.9.17		A.D.V.S. 30 Can Div. inspected the saloon, 3 admral deliveral.	
	25.9.17		Sectional duties visited my unit	
	26.9.17		Sectional duties, visited Machine Gun Squadron	
	27.9.17		Sectional duties visited my unit	

L. J. H.

WAR DIARY
or
INTELLIGENCE SUMMARY

Army Form C. 2118.

14 K. W. Nth Northumbryan San. September 1917 sheet 11 b

Place	Date	Hour	Summary of Events and Information	Remarks and references to Appendices
BOURS	29.9.17		Evacuated 3 sick cases and no urgent case to No 22 Stationary Hospital from S.T.P.O.L. sent ambulance train.	
	29.9.17		Sick and duties rendered by unit.	
	30.9.17		Sick and duties rendered by unit. Strength return for the month.	

L. Macaulay
Capt. A.D.C.
O.C. 1st. M.V.S.

14 Mob Vet[erinary] Sec[tion]
October 1917
Sheet 1117.

WAR DIARY
or
INTELLIGENCE SUMMARY.

Army Form C. 2118.

1st K Mobile Veterinary Section

Instructions regarding War Diaries and Intelligence Summaries are contained in F. S. Regs., Part II. and the Staff Manual respectively. Title pages will be prepared in manuscript.

Place	Date	Hour	Summary of Events and Information	Remarks and references to Appendices
BOURS	1.10.17		Sectional duties, visited my units	
	2.10.17		Admitted horses for evacuation, sectional duties visited my units	
	3.10.17		Evacuated sance cast horses to No 22 Vety Hospital sect all duties.	1.
	4.10.17		Sectional duties, visited my units	
	5.10.17		" " " "	
	6.10.17		" " " "	
	7.10.17		" " " "	
	8.10.17		" " " "	
	9.10.17		Section was packed up for the move on to following day, sectional duties	
	10.10.17		Section moved to the CALONNE – ROBECQ side, mer and horses rested under cover.	
Headquarters at CALONNE on LALONNE ROBECQ road	11.10.17		Sectional duties, visited B de A? OK, and # C.F.A.	
	12.10.17		Evacuated two cast horses to No 22 Vety Hospital from LA GORGUE through the 13 M.V.S.	2.
	13.10.17		A.D.V.S. and J.D.V.S. car Cowps inspected the sections sectional duties.	

WAR DIARY / INTELLIGENCE SUMMARY

Unit: 1/1 H.H. Yeomanry Section
Month/Year: October 1917
Sheet: 11 B

Place	Date	Hour	Summary of Events and Information	Remarks and references to Appendices
Hd.Qtrs. S CALONNE on CALONNE ROBECQ road.	17.10.17		Sectional duties.	
	18.10.17		A.D.M.S. inspected the cart and horses for evacuation.	
	18.10.17		Evacuated 8 sick men to 2. Infy. Hospital from LA GORGUE.	B
	19.10.17		Sectional duties rendering aid.	
	19.10.17		Evacuated 25 sick men one cart horse and 4 mules to 2 Infy. Hospital at LA GORGUE. Most of these men were sent to me from 4th 13th Yorks Infy. Section as they were moving.	25, 1, 4
	20.10.17		Sectional duties rendering my return again large.	
	21.10.17			
	22.10.17		Section moved to SAINS-LES-PERNES. Section moved at 12.45 pm and Bedlam short of forwards in advance until D.M.S. car left. On their arrival on advance to find billets, men and horses very fit indoor care.	
	23.10.17		Section moved to HOUVIN-HOUVIGNEUL. Section arrived at 12.15 pm.	

L.H.

WAR DIARY or INTELLIGENCE SUMMARY

14th K. Hotels Volunteers. October 1917 Sheet No 9

Army Form C. 2118.

Place	Date	Hour	Summary of Events and Information	Remarks and references to Appendices
	23.10.17		Breakfast served at 7.30 am and horses watered	
	24.10.17		Section moved to FIEFFES, horses and men are put fully groomed. Horses were put in the lines	
FIEFFES	25.10.17		Sectional duties carried out during the day	
"	26.10.17		"	
	27.10.17		Sectional duties, under orders of the Staff Capt. I had to find billets for section in RIBEAUCOURT and failed the village was occupied by cavalry. Similar results in BARLETTE & in turn by a troop of heavy cavalry in German	
	30.10.17		Section moved to FRANQUEVILLE (K 4) billets for horses. It was reported by H/ A.D.S. OD D.V.S. arrived at 11.15 shortly afterwards. Sectional duties carried out.	
	31.10.17		"	

Arrangements Knowles
H.L. Stammy
Capt. A.V.C.

WAR DIARY or INTELLIGENCE SUMMARY

Army Form C. 2118.

1st K. Mobile Veterinary Section

November 1917

Sheet No. 1
No. 130

Vol 33

Place	Date	Hour	Summary of Events and Information	Remarks and references to Appendices
FRANQUEVILLE				
FRANKEVILLES	1.11.17		A.D.V.S. inspected the section, inspected the 1st C.F.A. horse lines. Men were inspected for scabies. Pte 2839 Stanley F.W. was sent to Capt Walker A.V.C. to proceed to Can Infantry Corps School for duty.	
	2.11.17		Took over veterinary agenda of 1st M.G.B., Kislay, R.H.H, 1st CFA. E.Bde A.S.L.O.G.	
	3.11.17		Sectional duties.	
	4.11.17		A.D.V.S. inspected a weather mange case at FRANSU, visited of M.G. Sqn.	
	5.11.17		Sectional duties.	
	6.11.17		Sectional duties, visited my units.	
	7.11.17		D.V.S. inspected the section and sub horses, visited 1st M.G. Sqdt and sent one horse of the unit by Can Corps motor float to 2 Vety Hospital. A.D.V.S inspected the arrangements and ambulance conductance of the section. Evacuated 5 sub horses to 2 Vety Hospital, visited 12 R.V.S	
	8.11.17		Sectional duties visited my units.	
	9.11.17	"		
	10.11.17	"		

G. C. H.

13th Mobile Veterinary Section

WAR DIARY or **INTELLIGENCE SUMMARY**

March 1917 Sheet No. 131

Army Form C. 2118.

Place	Date	Hour	Summary of Events and Information	Remarks and references to Appendices
FRANQUEVILLE				
FRANKEVILLE	12.11.17		A.D.V.S. inspected the sick horses for evacuation, sectional duties.	
	13.11.17		Evacuated 1 sick horse from C AND A's station to 2 Vety Hospital at Abbeville. Evacuated one sick horse by motor float to 22 Vety Hospital sectional duties.	12.
	14.11.17		Sectional duties went to see A.D.V.S.	
	15.11.17		Sectional duties inspected my mules for a visit to lymphangitis	
	16.11.17		Admitted 62 sick horses for evacuation. 15+ we exposed to lymphangitis in isolated area.	
	17.11.17		Evacuated 66 sick horses to No 22 Vety Hospital at Abbeville by road on the long motor float. Also 15 of the 30 M.V.S. Section moved to LAHOUSSOYE it left at 4.50 p.m. and arrived at 10.45 p.m., the night was extraordinarily dark, men and horses were put under cover.	
	18.11.17		Section moved to CHUIGNEVILLES arrived at 9 p.m. men and horses were put under cover.	
	19.11.17		Sectional duties prepare to move on the following day, visited my unit.	
	20.11.17		Section started to form 7 horses 6.30 a.m. + 3 slow horses were disposed with 15th Lyc.	

G.C.H.

WAR DIARY
INTELLIGENCE SUMMARY

1/1 Noble Kauwery Section

November 1917

Army Form C. 2118.

Sheet No. 1 ₂₂

Place	Date	Hour	Summary of Events and Information	Remarks and references to Appendices
CHUIGNEULLES	21.11.17		Section stood to till 9 pm when it was ordered till 6.30 am on following day.	
	22.11.17		" " " " from 6.30 am at the water	
	23.11.17		Section moved from CHUIGNEULLES to LA HOUSSOYE arriving Pulalan at 3.45 pm and Beaulieu at 5.15 pm. Men and horses fed under now.	
LA HOUSSOYE	24.11.17		Sectional duties.	
	25.11.17		" "	
	26.11.17		" "	
	27.11.17		" "	
	28.11.17		Evacuated 11 sick horses from BELLE EGLISE to 22 Vety Hospital	
	29.11.17		Sectional duties.	
	30.11.17		Sectional duties stood to at 6.15 pm at 5 pm natives.	

Diary closed for the month.

G. C. Harding
Captain A.V.C.

WAR DIARY
INTELLIGENCE SUMMARY

Army Form C. 2118.

12th Mobile Veterinary Section

December 1917. Sheet 153.

Place	Date	Hour	Summary of Events and Information	Remarks and references to Appendices
LA HOUSSOYE	1.12.17		Sectional duties. Received orders in the evening to move to FRANVILLERS.	
	2.12.17		Section moved to FRANVILLERS. Sectional duties. Sent a division party to DAOURS	
FRANVILLERS	3.12.17		A.D.V.S. inspected the section and sick horses for evacuation. Sent 1 Cpl and 1 man to disinfect stables at DAOURS.	
	4.12.17		Evacuated 1 sick horse from BELLE EGLISE to No. 14 Vety Hospital ABBEVILLE. Sectional duties.	
	5.12.17		Sectional duties	
	6.12.17		do	
	7.12.17		do	
	8.12.17		do	
	9.12.17		do	
	10.12.17		Evacuated 16 horses to lymphangitis Contact camp. 2nd half Granted to No. 14 Vety Hospital from BELLE EGLISE. Sectional duties.	
	11.12.17		Evacuated 3 sick horses and 1 mule from ALBERT to No. 14 Vety Hospital FORGES LES EAUX. Sectional duties. G.C.H.	

13th Middlesex Bearer Section.   December 1917   Army Form C. 2118.

WAR DIARY
or
INTELLIGENCE SUMMARY.

Sheet 12.4

(Erase heading not required.)

Place	Date	Hour	Summary of Events and Information	Remarks and references to Appendices
FRANVILLERS	12/12		Sectional duties.	
	13/12		do	
	14/12		do.	
	15/12		Evacuated 10 Erysipelas, Lymphangitis, Contacts one case from ALBERT, 2nd life guards to No 7 Stay Hospital FORGES les EAUX Sectional duties	
	1/12		Sectional duties. A.D.V.S. inspected the section	
	4/12		Sectional duties	
	16/12		Evacuated 6 sick here to No 7 Stay Hospital FORGES les EAUX from ALBERT. Sectional duties	
			Sectional duties	
	19/12		do	
	20/12		do	
	21/12		do.	
	23/12		Section moved to BARLETTE started at 8.45 am and arrived at 5 pm. The journey was very hard owing to much snow and frozen roads, men and mules put with us.	
				G. C. H.

2333 Wt. W3311/1454 700,000 5/15 D. D. & L.   A.D.S.S./Forms/C. 2118.

WAR DIARY or INTELLIGENCE SUMMARY

Army Form C. 2118.

1st Mobile Veterinary Section

December 1915
Sheet 12 5.

Place	Date	Hour	Summary of Events and Information	Remarks and references to Appendices
BARLETTE	23/12/1		Sectional duties took over veterinary charge of 7th Cavalry Brigade Head Quarters	
	24/12/1		Sectional duties. Took over charge of 7th Machine Gun Squadron rested the unit in the afternoon.	
	25/12/1		Sectional duties.	
	26/12/1		Sectional duties, repacked all horses of the 7th Machine Gun Squadron	
	27/12/1		do. unfasted all horses of 7th Cavalry Brigade & Quakers.	
	28/12/1		Section moved to FRANSU, A.D.V.S. called in the morning	
	29/12/1		Evacuated B sick horses to No 14 Vety Hospital ABBEVILLE by road sectional duties.	
	30/12/1		Sectional duties.	
	31/12/1		Sectional duties, visited H.Q. of 7th Machine Gun Squadron	

Draw cheese for the month.

G. C. Hawkins
Capt. A.V.C.

12 K Noble Veterinary Section

WAR DIARY or INTELLIGENCE SUMMARY.

Army Form C. 2118.

January 1918   Sheet 126   Vol 35

Place	Date	Hour	Summary of Events and Information	Remarks and references to Appendices
FRANSU	1.1.18		Sectional duties. Visited Divisional School at BERNAVILLE Inspected of K Machine Gun Squadron. Met A.D.V.S. at LEPTOVY to see some Indian sufferers mange cases. Sent Cpl. E. ? men to disinfect stables of 2nd life Guards at ST GRATIEN.	
	3.1.18		Sectional duties. Inspected of K Cav Bde M.G. O.C. Visited Divisional School in the afternoon	
	4.1.18		Sectional duties. There was a fire at FRANSU the section turned out and helped to extinguish it during the night	
	5.1.18		Sectional duties. Visited the Divisional School	
	6.1.18		Sectional duties. A.D.V.S. called. Horse 13 M.V.S. Veterinary Hospital by road via 13 M.V.S.	
	7.1.18		Sectional duties. Visited Bde M.G. of A Machine Gun Squadron and Divisional School	
	8.1.18		Sectional duties.	
	9.1.18		Inspected of Machine Gun Squadron	
	10.1.18		Inspected 2nd Life Guards details. Divisional School Bde M.G. O.C. G.A.	

WAR DIARY or **INTELLIGENCE SUMMARY**

No 5 Mobile Veterinary Section

January 1918   Sheet 1

Army Form C. 2118.

Place	Date	Hour	Summary of Events and Information	Remarks and references to Appendices
FRANSU	11.1.18		Sectional duties	
	12.1.18		"	
	13.1.18		"	
	14.1.18		" evacuated 1 horse and 2 mules to No 1st Veterinary Hospital	12, 2
	15.1.18		" evacuated but evacuated 15 horses and 3 mules cast by D.R. sent by road to No 1 Veterinary Hospital	
	16.1.18		Sectional duties	
	17.1.18		Sectional duties, inspected R.A.H.Q.C referred Divisional School daily routine	
	18.1.18		"	
	19.1.18		"	
	20.1.18		"	
	21.1.18		A.D.V.S. visited the section in the afternoon and authorised for evacuation	1 & 3
	22.1.18		evacuated 1st horses and 2 mules to No 1st Veterinary Hospital by road, one horse was sent in lorry mule	
	23.1.18		Sectional duties	

E. C. Blr

WAR DIARY
INTELLIGENCE SUMMARY

1st K. Nob. Veterinary Section

January 1918

Sheet 1 of 6

Army Form C. 2118

Place	Date	Hour	Summary of Events and Information	Remarks and references to Appendices
FRANSU	23.1.18		Section at duties	
"	24.1.18			
"	25.1.18			
"	26.1.18			
"	27.1.18		A.D.V.S & D.D.V.S inspected the section in the morning. A.D.V.S came here for ammunition bus at Fransu.	
"	28.1.18		Travelled to No 14 Veterinary Hospital by road. 1 Epizootic lymphangitis Contact cast [1st Life Guards]	
"	29.1.18		To No 14 Veterinary Hospital by road.	
"	30.1.18		Section moved from FRANSU to PICQUIGNY started at 6.15am and arrived 10.15am. Echelon B echelon at 10.30am.	
"	31.1.18		Section marched to MARCELCAVE arrived at 3.15pm. Diary closed for the month. E. C. Wardman Capt R.A.V.C.	

14th Mobile Veterinary Section WAR DIARY February 1918 Army Form C. 2118.
or
INTELLIGENCE SUMMARY.

Steel 129

Place	Date	Hour	Summary of Events and Information	Remarks and references to Appendices
	1.2.18		Section moved to TREFCON, men were put in huts and horses under cover	
TREFCON	2.2.18		Routine duties	
"	3.2.18		" "	
"	4.2.18		" "	
"	5.2.18		" "	
"	6.2.18		" "	
"	7.2.18		" "	
"	8.2.18		Evacuated 3 sick horses to No 1 Vety Hospital from TINCOURT	3
"	9.2.18		Routine duties	
"	10.2.18		" "	
"	11.2.18		" "	
"	12.2.18		Evacuated one sick horse via 20 M.V.S. to No 7 Vety Hospital	1
"	13.2.18		Routine duties	
"	14.2.18		" "	
"	15.2.18		Evacuated 4 sick horses to No 7 Vety Hospital via 12 M.V.S	4

E. C. H.

14th Mobile Veterinary Section

WAR DIARY or INTELLIGENCE SUMMARY.

Army Form C. 2118.
Sheet 130.9
February 1918.

Place	Date	Hour	Summary of Events and Information	Remarks and references to Appendices
TREFCON	17/2/18		Took over duties from Capt. Hardey. Retained dutiks & arrived with	
	18/2/18		sick dutiks with war 132 Hy. R.G.A. & sick mule -	
	19/2/18		Sick duties & arrived mule - Visited by A.D.V.S. 3rd Cav. Div.	
	20/2/18		do	
	21/2/18		do	
	22/2/18		do Evacuated 12 horses + 3 mules	
			1. Q. 7. V.A. from TINCOURT	
	23/2/18		Sick duties & arrived mule -	
	24/2/18		do Visited by A.D.V.S. 3rd Cav. Div.	
	25/2/18		do	
	26/2/18		do	
	27/2/18		do	
	28/2/18		do	
	1/3/18		to Visited by A.D.V.S. 3rd Cav.	

E. C. Harding
Capt. A.V.C.

14th K Noble Veterinary Section

WAR DIARY
or
INTELLIGENCE SUMMARY.
(Erase heading not required.)

March 1918
Sheet 1 of 1

Army Form C. 2118

Vol 37

Instructions regarding War Diaries and Intelligence Summaries are contained in F. S. Regs., Part II and the Staff Manual respectively. Title pages will be prepared in manuscript.

Place	Date	Hour	Summary of Events and Information	Remarks and references to Appendices
TREFCON	2/3/18		Medium duties & evacuation	
"	3/3/18		"	
"	4/3/18		"	
"	5/3/18		Visited by D.D.V.S. in a.m. Inspected sick horses to be evacuated to Vety. Hospital from TINCOURT. Pronounced unfit. Hecke, Capt. R.A.V.C.	
"	6.3.18		1 horse to No. 7 Vety. Hospital from Capt. G. L. Harding	
"	7.3.18		Routine duties	
"	8.3.18		Routine duties	
"	9.3.18		Evacuated 1 sick horse from TINCOURT to No 7 Vety. Hospital 23	
"	10.3.18		Routine duties; was in veterinary charge of all the Brigade. Routine duties. Graze taken Cavalry wagon were mounted and ridden by the 1st Lancers, 6th Dragoons, 7th Dragoon Guards & the Machine Gun Squadron	
"	11.3.18		Routine duties	
"	12.3.18		Evacuated 2 sick horses from TINCOURT to No 7 Vety. Hospital 24. Section moved to MEREAUCOURT etc etc here billets from 26 M.V.S.	
"	13.3.18			G.L.H

WAR DIARY or INTELLIGENCE SUMMARY.

1st N. Midd. Vet. Cavalry Section   March 1918   Sheet 132

Army Form C. 2118.

Place	Date	Hour	Summary of Events and Information	Remarks and references to Appendices
MEREAUCOURT	13/3/18		Routine duties	
"	15/3/18		"	
"	16/3/18		"	
"	1/3/18		Section moved to ST CHRIST and took over billets previously	
ST CHRIST	18/3/18		occupied by the 10. M.V.S.	
"	19/3/18		Routine duties	
"	20/3/18		Evacuated eight sick men from LA CHAPELETTE	
"	21/3/18		Routine duties	
"	22/3		Section moved to BEAUMONT en BAISNE 5 men were	
"	23/3		put under orders there were billetted outside	
"	23/3/18		Moved to BRETIGNY routine duties	
CARLEPONT	24/3/18		Moved to a field near CARLEPONT sectional duties	
	25/3/18		Routine duties	
	26/3/18		Moved to a chateau near OLLENCOURT bivouacked	
			Moved to C.O.15 Van BACK, all Bewlays were divisionalised	

GC
14

14th Mobile Veterinary Section

WAR DIARY
of
INTELLIGENCE SUMMARY

March 1918   Sheet 133

Army Form C. 2118

Instructions regarding War Diaries and Intelligence Summaries are contained in F. S. Regs. Part II. and the Staff Manual respectively. Title pages will be prepared in manuscript.

Place	Date	Hour	Summary of Events and Information	Remarks and references to Appendices
	26/3/18		Received orders to proceed to LES-CLOYES with section and one V.O. of Canadian Cavalry Brigade. Started at 9 p.m.	
	27/3/18		Arrived 11.50 p.m. reported to A.D.V.S. 2nd Cav. Div. Section returned to CHOISY au BACK and bivouacked for the night.	
CHOISY au BACK	28/3/18		Stood to all day.	
	29/3/18		Section moved to the AVRECHY area, and bivouacked for the night.	
	30/3/18		Moved to LA RACINOUS Fm near SAINS EN AMENOIS and bivouacked for the night.	
SAINS EN AMENOIS	31/3/18		Stood to all day. Routine duties.	

Diary closed for the month.
G. Harding
Capt A.V.C.
O.C. 14th M.V.S.

Mob. Vet. Veterinary Section.   April 1918.   Army Form C. 2118.
Sheet 134.

Vol 38

WAR DIARY
or
INTELLIGENCE SUMMARY.
(Erase heading not required.)

Place	Date	Hour	Summary of Events and Information	Remarks and references to Appendices
	1.4.18		Section moved to S.18.d in N.E. edge of the BOIS de BOVES, this section was amalgamated with the 13.M.V.S. received 9 horses & 1 mule collected by the 13.M.V.S.	Reference Map 62D 9.1.
	2.4.18		Evacuated 11 horses & 1 mule from SALEUX, these horses and mule were taken to hospital by A/Cpl Stanton of 13.M.V.S. Section moved to BLANGY-TRONVILLE, men and horses were put under cover	11.1.
	3.4.18		Evacuated 29 horses from SALEUX, these were collected from Echelon B at PONT de METZ	2.9.
	4.4.18		Received orders from A.D.V.S. 6th Cav Div to proceed to x roads about 1 mile S.E. of FOUILLOY with 10 mounted men to collect sick. At 10.45 p.m. received orders from A.D.V.S. 6th Cav Div to return to BLANGY-TRONVILLE where the remainder of the section was billeted	
	5.4.18		Evacuated 37 horses via the Canadian M.V.S. at SALEUX	37
	6.4.18		Section moved to LAMOTTE-BREBIERE and joined the r/ the Cav. Bde. The horses were picqueted in the open, the men were billeted in Nissen Huts.	

G. C. H.

1st K. Nathlakturay Section April 1918   Army Form C. 2118.
Sheet 135.

WAR DIARY
INTELLIGENCE SUMMARY
(Erase heading not required.)

Instructions regarding War Diaries and Intelligence Summaries are contained in F.S. Regs., Part II. and the Staff Manual respectively. Title pages will be prepared in manuscript.

Place	Date	Hour	Summary of Events and Information	Remarks and references to Appendices
	7/4/18		Evacuated 30 horses and 3 mules via 1st Canadian M.V.S.	20, 2.
	8/4/18		SALEUX Evacuated 30 horses via 1st Canadian M.V.S.	20.
	9/4/18		Sectional duties.	
	10/4/18		Section moved to ARGOEUVES.	
	11/4/18		Section moved to OCCOCHES arrived at 6.15 pm men and horses went full under cover. Bivouac was dis-crowded under the orders of the O.C. A.S.C. at LONG. 1 Sick horse accompanied it	13.
	12/4/18		Received orders about 12 noon to stand to at 3 hrs notice. Later section moved to ST MARTIN L'EGLISE arrived 8 to 9 pm men and horses were but under cover.	
	13/4/18		Section moved to FLORINGHEM and stood to at 1 hrs notice. In evening section moved back to VALHUON and found billets.	
	14/4/18		Saddled up at 7.0 am in accordance with orders and off saddled shortly afterwards. Section moved to BOURS and found billets.	
	15/4/18		Section moved to HANQUEVILLE and found billets, evacuated 8 horses.	

E.C.H.

14th Mobile Veterinary Section   April 1918   Army Form C. 2118.
                                   sheet 1 & 2

WAR DIARY
or
INTELLIGENCE SUMMARY

(Erase heading not required.)

Place	Date	Hour	Summary of Events and Information	Remarks and references to Appendices
	15.4.18		from ST. POL.	
	16.4.18		Stood by at MANQUEVILLE, moved back to BOURS in the afternoon to reobillet.	
BOURS	17.4.18		Sectional duties.	
	18.4.18		Sectional duties.	
	19.4.18		Evacuated 2 horses from PERNES station to No 13 Vety. Hospital	2/1.
	20.4.18		Sectional duties.	
	21.4.18		Evacuated 12 horses from PERNES station to No 18 Vety. Hospital	12.
	22.4.18		Sectional duties.	
	23.4.18		Evacuated 7 horses and 1 mule from PERNES station to No 13 Vety Hospital	7/1.
	24.4.18		Sectional duties.	
	25.4.18		"	
	26.4.18		"	
	27.4.18		Inspection of this section was imparted by the O.C. A.S.C. and M.D.V.S. All horses transport teams here in full marching order as ordered. I'm unaware by G.O.C. of K. Can Bde., he was unable to attend. E.C.H.

1st Mobile Veterinary Section.   April 1918.   Army Form C. 2118.
Sheet 13 of /.

WAR DIARY
or
INTELLIGENCE SUMMARY.
(Erase heading not required.)

Instructions regarding War Diaries and Intelligence Summaries are contained in F. S. Regs., Part II. and the Staff Manual respectively. Title pages will be prepared in manuscript.

Place	Date	Hour	Summary of Events and Information	Remarks and references to Appendices
BOURS	28.4.18		Evacuated 19 horses to No 12 Vety Hospital from PERNES	19.
	29.4.18		Evacuated 3 horses from PERNES to No 12 Vety Hospital	3.
	30.4.18		Sent usual return.	
			Diary closed for the month	
			G. C. Harding	
			Capt A.V.C.	
			O.C. 1st M.V.S.	

14th Mobile Veterinary Section   WAR DIARY   May 26th – 31st inclusive   Army Form C. 2118.
or
INTELLIGENCE SUMMARY.   1918.
(Erase heading not required.)   Sheet 138.   M 39

Place	Date	Hour	Summary of Events and Information	Remarks and references to Appendices
Montigny	26.5.18		Took over command of 14th M.V.S. at Montigny from Capt Parsons. C.A.V.C. and reported arrival at Bde Hd Qrs. Visited all units with Capt Parsons.	
	27.5.18		Capt. Parsons C.A.V.C. left Montigny at 6.30. A.M. to rejoin his unit. Sectional duties – visited my unit	
	28.5.18		Evacuated 10 Horses & 1 Mule by rail from Paulainville to No 15. V.H. Sectional duties Visited by Capt Ryan A.V.C., acting for A.D.V.S. 3rd Cav. Div.	
	29.5.18		Sectional duties – visited my units	
	30.5.18		Sectional duties – visited my units Section moved to Belloy sur Somme – took over billets from 13th M.V.S.	
	31.5.18		Handed over 6 Horses to 13th M.V.S. at Montigny.	

Diary closed for the month

Sturgill Lt. A.V.C.
O.C. 14th M.V.S.

44th Mobile Veterinary Section

Army Form C. 2118.

WAR DIARY

June 1918.

Sheet 139

(Erase heading not required)

Place	Date	Hour	Summary of Events and Information	Remarks and references to Appendices
BELLOY Sur SOMME.	1/6/18		Sectional Duties – visited my unit	
"	2/6/18		do.	
"	3/6/18		Evacuated 4 Horses to XIX V.E.S. at PICQUIGNY. – Sectional duties	
"	4/6/18		" 2 " " " " "	
"	5/6/18		Visited by D.D.V.S. Cav. Corps – Sectional duties, visited my unit.	
"	6/6/18		Evacuated 2 Horses to XIX V.E.S. at PICQUIGNY. – Sectional duties	
"	7/6/18		Sectional duties – visited my unit	
"	8/6/18		Evacuated 1 Horse to XIX V.E.S. at PICQUIGNY. – Sectional duties	
"	9/6/18		" 2 " " " " "	
"	10/6/18		Sectional duties, visited my unit	
"	11/6/18		Evacuated 4 Horses to XIX V.E.S. at PICQUIGNY. – Sectional duties	
"	12/6/18		" 10 " " " " " four of which were cast by D.D.R.	
"	13/6/18		Veterinary cases, and six Remount cases, cast by D.D.R. Sectional duties, visited my unit Evacuated 4 Horses to XIX V.E.S. at PICQUIGNY – Sectional duties, visited my unit – Evacuated 2 Horses to XIX V.E.S. at PICQUIGNY same afternoon.	

Army Form C. 2118.

WAR DIARY
or
INTELLIGENCE SUMMARY.

(Erase heading not required.)

14th Mobile Veterinary Section.   June 1918 (Contd.)

Sheet 140

Instructions regarding War Diaries and Intelligence Summaries are contained in F.S. Regs., Part II. and the Staff Manual respectively. Title pages will be prepared in manuscript.

Place	Date	Hour	Summary of Events and Information	Remarks and references to Appendices
BELLOY-SUR-SOMME.	14/6/18		Section moved to MONTIGNY + took over Billets evacuated by 13th M.V.S. - also took charge of 2 Horses (sick) left by 13th M.V.S.	
MONTIGNY.	15/6/18		Visited by D.D.V.S. Cav. Corps and A.D.V.S. 3rd Cav. Div. — Sectional duties, visited units.	
"	16/6/18		Sectional duties – visited units	
"	17/6/18		do.	
"	18/6/18		Evacuated 8 Horses from PAULAINVILLE to No 15 Veterinary Hospital – Sectional duties, visited units.	
"	19/6/18		do.	
"	20/6/18		do.	
"	21/6/18		Evacuated 6 Horses from PAULAINVILLE to No 15. Veterinary Hospital	
"	22/6/18		Section moved to St OWEN took over billets evacuated by 'A' C.M.V.S. - also took over 2 Horses (sick) left by 'A' C.M.V.S.	
St OWEN	23/6/18		Sectional duties – visited units	
"	24/6/18		do	
"	25/6/18		Evacuated 6 Horses at St LEGER ce DOMART for 15 Veterinary Hospital	

14th Mobile Veterinary Section   JUNE 1918 (Cont) Army Form C. 2118.

WAR DIARY
or
INTELLIGENCE SUMMARY.

Sheet 141

Place	Date	Hour	Summary of Events and Information	Remarks and references to Appendices
St OWEN	25/6/18		Visited by A.D.V.S. 3rd Cav. Div – Sectional duties – visited unit	
"	26/6/18		Sectional duties – visited my unit.	
"	27/6/18		A.D.V.S. 3rd Cav Div - held his monthly inspection of Section – visited my unit.	
"	28/6/18		Evacuated 4 Horses & 2 Mules at St LEGER to DOMARTS from No 15 Veterinary Hospital	
"	29/6/18		Sectional duties – visited my unit	
"	30/6/18		do	
			do	

Diary closed for the month.

6/18

Sanghill Capt
Capt. A.V.C.
O. C. 14th Mobile Veterinary Section

714th Mobile Veterinary Section

Army Form C. 2118.

WAR DIARY
or
INTELLIGENCE SUMMARY.

July 1918

Sheet 14γ

VA 31

Place	Date	Hour	Summary of Events and Information	Remarks and references to Appendices
OUEN	1.7.18		Section duties - visited my units	
"	2.7.18		Evacuated 5 Horses + 1 Mule at S¹ LEGER les DOMARTS for 15 Veterinary Hospital	
"	3.7.18		Section duties - visited my unit	
"	4.7.18		do.	
"	5.7.18		do. A.D.V.S. visited section	
"	6.7.18		do.	
"	7.7.18		do.	
"	8.7.18		do.	
"	9.7.18		Evacuated 6 Horses + 1 Mule at S¹ LEGER les DOMARTS for 15 Veterinary Hospital	
"	10.7.18		Section duties - visited my units	
"	11.7.18		do.	
"	12.7.18		Evacuated 2 Horses at S¹ LEGER les DOMART for XV Veterinary Hospital	
"	13.7.18		Section duties - visited my unit	
"	14.7.18		do	
"	15.7.18		do	
"	16.7.18		do A.D.V.S. visited Section	

"14" Mobile Veterinary Section. WAR DIARY or INTELLIGENCE SUMMARY. JULY 1918 (cont) Army Form C. 2118.

Sheet 143

Place	Date	Hour	Summary of Events and Information	Remarks and references to Appendices
St OUEN	17.7.18		Section duties - visited my unit	
"	18.7.18		do.	
"	19.7.18		Evacuated 8 Horses at St LEGER les DOMARTS for XV Veterinary Hospital	
"	20.7.18		Section duties - visited my unit	
"	21.7.18		do.	
"	22.7.18		do.	
"	23.7.18		do. D.D.V.S visited Section	
"	24.7.18		do.	
"	25.7.18		do. A.D.V.S visited Section	
"	26.7.18		do.	
"	27.7.18		do.	
"	28.7.18		do.	
"	29.7.18		do. A.D.V.S inspected Section	
"	30.7.18		do.	
"	31.7.18		Evacuated 5 Horses to No XIX V.E.S. PICQUIGNY	

Diary closed for the month. [signature] Capt. O.C. 14 M.V.S.
5/8/18

14 Mob Vety Sect
August 1918
Sheet No 144.

WAR DIARY
INTELLIGENCE SUMMARY

14. Mobile Veterinary Section,

Place	Date	Hour	Summary of Events and Information	Remarks and references to Appendices
ST OUEN	1.8/18		Section duties – visited my units	
do	2.8/18		do	
do	3.8/18		do	
do	4.8/18		do	
do	5.8/18		Evacuated 5 Horses + 7 Mules to XIX VES. PICQUIGNY – ADVS. visited Section	
do			Section moved to BOURDON	
BOURDON	6.8/18		Evacuated 6 Horses + 1 Mule to XIX V.E.S. PICQUIGNY – ADVS visited Section	
			Section moved to MONTIÈRES area.	
Pont de METZ	7.8/18		Section moved to Pont de METZ – Evacuated 1 Horse to 13.M.V.S. at SALEUX	
BOVES	8.8/18		Section moved to BOVES.	
do	9.8/18		Evacuated 51 Horses + 2 Mules to 13 M.V.S. at SALEUX	
DOMART sur la LUCE	10.8/18		Section moved to DOMART sur la LUCE – took over 118 animals from 'A' Canadian M.V.S.	
do	11/9/18		Evacuated 104 Horses + 3 Mules to 13 M.V.S. at BOVES.	
do			Evacuated 48 Horses to 13 M.V.S. at BOVES	
do	12.9/18		Evacuated 51 Horses + 5 Mules to 13 M.V.S. at BOVES.	

4 Mobile Veterinary Section   August 1918 (cont.) Army Form C. 2118.

WAR DIARY
or
INTELLIGENCE SUMMARY

Sheet 145

Place	Date	Hour	Summary of Events and Information	Remarks and references to Appendices
GUYENCOURT	13/8/18		Section moved to GUYENCOURT rejoined 7th Cav. Bde.	
do	14/8/18		Evacuated 13 Horses to Canadian Corps. V.E.S at BOVES.	
do	15/8/18		Section duties - visited my unit	
St OUEN	16/8/18		Section moved to St OUEN	
do	17/8/18		Section duties - visited my unit	
do	18/8/18		do	
do	19/8/18		do	
do	20/8/18		Evacuated 10 Horses to XIX V.E.S. at PICQUIGNY	
do	21/8/18		Capt. G.K. Shaw. A.V.C. took over command of Section from Capt. B.A. M°HILL AVC whilst proceeded on leave to U.K.	
do	22/8/18		Evacuated 3 Horses to XIX V.E.S. Picquigny. D.D.V.S visited Section	
do	23/8/18		Section duties - visited my unit	
do	24/8/18		do	
do	25/8/18		Evacuated 10 Horses to XIX V.E.S. PICQUIGNY	
			Section moved to le BOISLE	

Shaw.

14 Mobile Veterinary Section

WAR DIARY
or
INTELLIGENCE SUMMARY

August 1918 (cont) Army Form C. 2118.
Sheet 146

Place	Date	Hour	Summary of Events and Information	Remarks and references to Appendices
LE BOISLE	26/8/18		Section moved to CONCHY SUR CANCHE	
Conchy Sur Cancke	27/8/18		Section duties - visited my units	
do	28/8/18		do	
do	29/8/18		do	
do	30/8/18		Evacuated 2 Horses to No 2 Veterinary Collecting Post at St POL. A.D.V.S. visited section	
do	31/8/18		Section duties - visited my units	

Diary closed for the month.

Scanfield Capt. a.v.c.
O.C. 14.M.V.S.

14. Mobile Veterinary Section

WAR DIARY or **INTELLIGENCE SUMMARY**

September 1918. Army Form C. 2118. Sheet 147

Place	Date	Hour	Summary of Events and Information	Remarks and references to Appendices
Conchy sur Canche	1.9.18		Section duties - visited unit	
"	3.9.18		do	
"	4.9.18		Evacuated 8 Horses to St Pol No 2 V.C.P.	
"	5.9.18		Section duties - A.D.V.S. visited Section	
"	6.9.18		Section duties - Capt B.A.Myhill A.V.C. returned from leave to U.K. took over Command of Section	
"	7.9.18	11 AM	Section moved to Boubers - Section duties	
Boubers	8.9.18		Section duties - visited units	
"	9.9.18		do	
"	10.9.18		Evacuated 3 Horses to No 2 V.C.P at St Pol - Section moved to Willeman	
Willeman	11.9.18		Section duties - A.D.V.S visited Section	
"	12.9.18		do - visited units.	
"	13.9.18		Evacuated 8 Horses to No 2 V.C.P at St Pol	
"	14.9.18		Section duties	
"	15.9.18		Evacuated 5 Horses to No 2 V.C.P at St Pol	
Rollencourt	16.9.18		Section moved to Rollencourt.	

14 Mobile Veterinary Section   September 1918 (cont.)   Army Form C. 2118.

WAR DIARY or INTELLIGENCE SUMMARY.
(Erase heading not required.)

Sheet 148

Place	Date	Hour	Summary of Events and Information	Remarks and references to Appendices
Field	17.9.18		Section took part in Cavalry Corps. field operations - arrived at MAIZICOURT 4:30pm.	
WILLEMAN	18.9.18		Section moved to WILLEMAN	
"	19.9.18		Section duties - visited unit	
"	20.9.18		do	
"	21.9.18		Evacuated 4 Horses to No 1 V.C.P. at St POL - Section duties	
"	22.9.18		Collected 1 Horse by float from St GEORGE'S. A.D.V.S visited Section	
"	23.9.18		Evacuated 4 Horses to No 1 V.C.P. at St POL - Section duties.	
"	24.9.18		" 14 " " " " "	
"	25.9.18		" 5 " " " " " - Section moved to ORVILLE	
ORVILLE	26.9.18		Section moved to SENLIS.	
SENLIS	27.9.18		" " " HEM	
HEM	28.9.18		Section duties - visited unit	
"	29.9.18		Evacuated 20 Horses to No 3 V.E.S at HAUT-ALLAINES - Section moved to VERMAND	
VERMAND	30.9.18		" 9 " " Australian V.E.S at TINCOURT.	

Diary closed for the month.

1/10/18.
[signature] Capt A.V.C.
O.C. 14. M.V.S

"14" Mobile Veterinary Section   October 1918   Army Form C. 2118.

WAR DIARY
or
INTELLIGENCE SUMMARY.

Sheet. 149

Place	Date	Hour	Summary of Events and Information	Remarks and references to Appendices
VERMAND	1.10.18		Section duties - visited unit.	
do	2.10.18		Evacuated 4 horses to No 2 M.V.S. at VERMAND	
do	3.10.18		do " 4 " " " "	
do	4.10.18		do " 1 " " " "	
do	5.10.18		do " " " " "	
do	6.10.18		Evacuated 3 Horses to "A" Canadian M.V.S. at VERMAND. Section moved thereon divisional at X roads R.6.c central (Sheet 62.C) - Section moved at 3 p.m. to La BARAQUE (62 g d central (Sheet 62b) - Section moved at 5.30 p.m. to VERMAND, + rejoined 7th Cavalry Brigade.	
do	7.10.18		Evacuated 8 Horses to "A" Canadian M.V.S. at VERMAND - Section moved to BELLENGLISE.	
do	8.10.18		Section moved at 8.30 am to S.W. MAGNY-LA-FOSSE" @ 30 b4.0. (62B) - Section moved at 11.30 E valley S.W. of JONCOURT HIS a 2.8. - Section moved at 1.30 pm to valley NE of ESTREES B 28 a.1.8. Section moved at 6 pm. to area H 14 c 9.8. - Evacuated 2 Horses to "A" Canadian M.V.S. at G 30 b 4.c (57B).	
1-?	9.10.18		Section moved at 6.30am to area NE of GENÊVE B18 a 9.8. - Section moved at 10 am to area S of MARETZ U 17 d 4.3. - Evacuated 51 Horses to 13 M.V.S. at X Roads U 21 d 6.9 (Sheet 57B)	
BERTRY	10.10.18		Section moved at 9 pm to area N.E of BERTRY Pq a 8.8 (Sheet 57B) - Evacuated 89 Horses to 13 M.V.S. at X roads U 21 d 6.9. Sheet 57B.	

14th Mobile Veterinary Section. October 1918 (cont.) Army Form C. 2118.

WAR DIARY
or
INTELLIGENCE SUMMARY.

Sheet 150.

Place	Date	Hour	Summary of Events and Information	Remarks and references to Appendices
BERTRY	11.10.18		Evacuated 40 Horses to 13 M.V.S. at X Roads. U.31d.6.9. Sheet 57.B.	
"	12.10.18		" " " 2 Mules to 13 M.V.S. " " — Section moved at 6.30 p.m.	
"	13.10.18		to area N.E. of CLARY. P.18.c.8.8. Sheet 57.B	
	14.10.18		Section rejoined 7th Cav. Bde. & moved at 9 a.m. to HONNECOURT — A.D.V.S. visited Section.	
BERTINCOURT	15.10.18		Section moved to BERTINCOURT — A.D.V.S. visited Section	
do	16.10.18		Section duties — Routine. visited units	
do	17.10.18		" "	
do	18.10.18		" — Evacuated 17 Horses to No 6. V.E.S. at MASNIERS.	
do	19.10.18		" "	
do	20.10.18		" — O.C. A.S.C. 3rd Cav. Div. inspected all transport.	
do	21.10.18		" "	
do	22.10.18		" — Evacuated 12 Horses to No 13 V.E.S. - ROISEL	
do	23.10.18		" "	
do	24.10.18		" "	
do	25.10.18		" "	

Signed.

14th Mobile Veterinary Section   October 1918 (cont)   Army Form C. 2118.

WAR DIARY
or
INTELLIGENCE SUMMARY.
(Erase heading not required.)

Sheet 151.

Place	Date	Hour	Summary of Events and Information	Remarks and references to Appendices
BERTINCOURT	26/10/18		Section duties - Routine - visited units.	
do	27/10/18		" " " " "	
do	28/10/18		" " " - Evacuated 15 Horses 1 Mule to No 6 V.E.S CAMBRAI.	
do	29/10/18		" " " - A.D.V.S. visited Section	
do	30/10/18		" " " " "	
do	31/10/18		" " " " "	

Diary closed for the month.

[signature]
Capt. A.V.C.
O.C. 14th Mobile Veterinary Section.

Army Form C. 2118.

14 Mobile Veterinary Section

WAR DIARY or INTELLIGENCE SUMMARY.

November 1918. Sheet 152.

(Erase heading not required.)

Place	Date	Hour	Summary of Events and Information	Remarks and references to Appendices
Bertincourt.	1/11/18		Routine work. visited units.	
"	2/11/18		do. — Evacuated 9 Horses to No 6 U.E.S. Cambrai.	
"	3/11/18		do.	
"	4/11/18		do.	
"	5/11/18		do.	
Sauchy-Cauchy	6/11/18		Section moved to Sauchy-Cauchy.	
Planque.	7/11/18		" " " Planque — Evacuated 1 Horse to No 18. V.E.S at Douai.	
Wahagnies.	8/11/18		" " " Wahagnies — " 1 Horse to no 3 V.E.S. at Senlis.	
"	9/11/18		" " " Tourcoing	
Tourcoing	10/11/18		Routine work. visited units — Evacuated 21 Horses + 1 Mule to No XV V.E.S. at Tourcoing.	
"	11/11/18		do. — do. 2 " to No XV V.E.S - Tourcoing	
"	12/11/18		do.	
"	13/11/18		do. — Evacuated 11 Horses to No XV V.E.S. at Tourcoing.	
"	14/11/18		do. — " 32 " " "	
"	15/11/18		do.	
Frasnes & Buissenal	16/11/18		Section moved to Frasnes & Buissenal.	
Moerbeke	17/11/18		" " " Moerbeke — Evacuated 1 Horse to 18. M.V.S. at Frasnes & Buissenal.	
Castre.	18/11/18		" " " Castre.	
"	19/11/18		Routine work. visited units.	
"	20/11/18		do. — Evacuated 12 Horses to "A" Canadian. M.V.S. at Grammont.	

Jones.

14th Mobile Veterinary Section.

WAR DIARY or **INTELLIGENCE SUMMARY.**

Army Form C. 2118.

November 1918 (cont.) Sheet 153.

Place	Date	Hour	Summary of Events and Information	Remarks and references to Appendices
RENIVAL.	21/11/18		Section moved to RENIVAL.	
MALEVES.	22/11/18		Section moved to MALEVES Ste MARIE-WASTINES.	
do	23/11/18		Routine work - visited units.	
JODINGE-SOUVERAIN	24/11/18		Section moved to JODINGE-SOUVERAINE.	
do	25/11/18		Routine work. visited units.	
do	26/11/18		do	
do	27/11/18		do	
do	28/11/18		do	
do	29/11/18		do	
do	30/11/18		do	

Diary closed for the month.

[signature]
Capt. A.V.C.
O.C. 14th Mobile Veterinary Section.

14th Mobile Veterinary Section   Army Form C. 2118.

Instructions regarding War Diaries and Intelligence
Summaries are contained in F. S. Regs., Part II.
and the Staff Manual respectively. Title pages
will be prepared in manuscript.

WAR DIARY
or
INTELLIGENCE SUMMARY.
(Erase heading not required.)

December 1918
Sheet 154.

Place	Date	Hour	Summary of Events and Information	Remarks and references to Appendices
JODOIGNE-SOUVERAINE	1/12/18		Routine work - visited units	
"	2/12/18		do	
"	3/12/18		do. A.D.V.S. visited Section	
"	4/12/18		do. - Evacuated 4 Horses to 13.M.V.S.	
"	5/12/18		do.	
"	6/12/18		do.	
"	7/12/18		do.	
"	8/12/18		do.	
"	9/12/18		do.	
"	10/12/18		do.	
"	11/12/18		do.	
"	12/12/18		do.	
"	13/12/18		do. Evacuated 6 Horses to Canadian V.E.S. at NAMUR.	
"	14/12/18		do.	
WARNANT.	15/12/18		Section moved to WARNANT.	
VIEN	16/12/18		" " VIEN.	
"	17/12/18		Routine work - visited units.	
"	18/12/18		do	
"	19/12/18		do	
"	20/12/18		do	
"	21/12/18		do	
"	22/12/18		do	

Army Form C. 2118.

14th Mobile Veterinary Section

WAR DIARY
or
~~INTELLIGENCE SUMMARY.~~

December 1918 (cont.)
Sheet 156.

Instructions regarding War Diaries and Intelligence Summaries are contained in F. S. Regs., Part II. and the Staff Manual respectively. Title pages will be prepared in manuscript.

(Erase heading not required.)

Place	Date	Hour	Summary of Events and Information	Remarks and references to Appendices
VIEN	23/12/18		Routine work - visited units.	
"	24/12/18		do	
"	25/12/18		do	
"	26/12/18		do. - D.D.V.S visited Section.	
"	27/12/18		do	
"	28/12/18		do	
"	29/12/18		do	
"	30/12/18		do.	
"	31/12/18		do. - Evacuated 7 Horses by rail to NEUFCHATEL	

Diary closed for month.

Scurfield Capt.
OC 14. M. V.S.

14d Mobile Veterinary Section.

WAR DIARY
or
INTELLIGENCE SUMMARY.

Army Form C. 2118.

January 1919
Sheet 157

Place	Date	Hour	Summary of Events and Information	Remarks and references to Appendices
VIEN.	1st		Routine work - visited units.	
	2nd		do	
	3rd		do	
	4th		do	
	5th		do	
	6th		do	
	7th		do - Evacuated 9 Horses 1 Mule to Neuf CHATEL.	
	8th		do	
	9th		do	
	10th		do	
	11th		do	
	12th		do	
	13th		do	
	14th		do	
	15th		do	
	16th		do. Evacuated 14 Horses 6 "A" Canadian. M.V.S. at La TOLLE	
	17th		do	
	18th		do. Evacuated 4 Horses 2 Mules to Advanced Vety. Hp. at CHARLEROI.	
	19th		do	
	20th		do	
	21st		do	
	22nd		do	
	23rd		do. Evacuated 14 Horses 16 "A" Canadian M.V.S. at La TOLLE	
	24th		do. Evacuated 1 Horse to 7th Can. Stle. - Routine work.	
	25th		do	
	26th		do	
	27th		On Board unit ADVS for Vety. Classification of animals in 7th Can. Stle.	
	28th		do	
	29th		do	
	30th		do	
	31st		do. Diary closed for the Month. Evacuated 3 Horses to "A" Canadian M.V.S at EHEIN.	

Irving Hall Capt
OC 14. MVS

M.D. Mobile Veterinary Section. 31   February 1919   Army Form C. 2118.

WAR DIARY
or
INTELLIGENCE SUMMARY.
(Erase heading not required.)

Instructions regarding War Diaries and Intelligence Summaries are contained in F. S. Regs., Part II. and the Staff Manual respectively. Title pages will be prepared in manuscript.

Sheet # 158.
Vol 49

Place	Date	Hour	Summary of Events and Information	Remarks and references to Appendices
VIEN.	1-2-19		Evacuated 15 Horses to "A" Canadian M.V.S.. Routine work	
"	2-2-19		Visited unit. Routine work	
"	3-2-19		do	
"	4-2-19		do	
"	5-2-19		do	
"	6-2-19		do	
"	7-2-19		Evacuated 21 Horses to "A" Canadian M.V.S. at EHEIN	
"	8-2-19		No sick unit. Routine work	
"	9-2-19		Evacuated 65 Horses to Advanced Veterinary Hospital at CHARLEROI.	
"	10-2-19		Visited units - Routine work	
"	11-2-19		do	
"	12-2-19		Evacuated 12 Horses to "A" Canadian M.V.S. at EHEIN	
"	13-2-19		Visited unit. Routine work	
"	14-2-19		Evacuated 16 Horses to "A" Canadian M.V.S. at EHEIN and 6 Horses to 13 M.V.S. at STOCRAK	
"	15-2-19		Visited units - Routine work.	
"	16-2-19		do	
"	17-2-19		do A.D.V.S. visited unit	
"	18-2-19		Evacuated 32 Horses & 1 Mule to Advanced Veterinary Hospital CHARLEROI.	
"	19-2-19		Visited unit - Routine work. Evacuated 1 Horse to "A" Canadian M.V.S. at EHEIN.	
"	20-2-19		do	
"	21-2-19		do	
"	22-2-19		do	

Seey.

Army Form C. 2118

14ᵗʰ Mobile Veterinary Section

WAR DIARY
or
INTELLIGENCE SUMMARY

February 1919 (cont). Sheet 159

(Erase heading not required.)

Instructions regarding War Diaries and Intelligence Summaries are contained in F. S. Regs., Part II. and the Staff Manual respectively. Title pages will be prepared in manuscript.

Place	Date	Hour	Summary of Events and Information	Remarks and references to Appendices
VIEN	23/2/19		Visited units – Routine work	
"	24/2/19		do. do.	
"	25/2/19		do. do.	
"	26/2/19		do. do.	
"	27/2/19		do. do.	
"	28/2/19		do. do.	

Diary closed for th month.

Bamfield Capt.

1/3/19 O.C. 14 M.V.S.

Army Form C. 2118

WAR DIARY
INTELLIGENCE SUMMARY.

(Erase heading not required.)

Instructions regarding War Diaries and Intelligence Summaries are contained in F.S. Regs., Part II. and the Staff Manual respectively. Title pages will be prepared in manuscript.

March 1919   14th M.S. Veky Sect.

Place	Date	Hour	Summary of Events and Information	Remarks and references to Appendices
VIEN	1st		A.D.V.S. visited section. Visited units & routine work.	
	2nd		Handed over S.C.t to Capt J.J. MILLS R.A.V.C.	
	3rd		Capt Myhill R.A.V.C. proceeded to U.K. on leave. Visited units & routine work.	
	4th		Visited units & routine work.	
	5th		" " "	
	6th		" " "	
	7th		" " "	
	8th		" " "	
	9th		Sold eight horses & 2 mules to butcher as unfit at LIEGE	
	10th		Evacuated 12 horses & 3 mules to Advanced Vety Hospital CHARLEROI.	
	11th		Visited units & routine work.	
NANDRIN	12th		Moved to NANDRIN.	
	13th		Visited units & routine work.	
	14th		" " "	
	15th		" " "	
	16th		" " "	
	17th		" " "	
	18th		" " "	
	19th		" " "	
	20th		Evacuated 3 horses to Z Depot SERAING for destruction. Routine work.	
	21st		Visited units & routine work.	

WAR DIARY
or
INTELLIGENCE SUMMARY.

Army Form C. 2118.

(Erase heading not required.)

14th Mob Vety Sect.

March 1919

Place	Date	Hour	Summary of Events and Information	Remarks and references to Appendices
NANDRIN	22		Visited units & routine work	
"	23		" " "	
"	24		" " "	
"	25		" " "	
"	26		" " "	
"	27		" " "	
"	28		Moved from NANDRIN to AMAY	
"	29th		Visited units & routine work	
"	30th		Reconctd & drove by road to advanced Vety Hospital DUREN	
"	31st		Routine work sawfish at Animal Abbey Corp ENGRS	

J.J. Mills
Capt R.A.V.C.
O.C. 14th M.V.S.

Volume 162 April

WAR DIARY
INTELLIGENCE SUMMARY.

Army Form C. 2118.

3/13th/4th Pro V Vety Sections

(Erase heading not required.)

Place	Date	Hour	Summary of Events and Information	Remarks and references to Appendices
AMAY	1st		Routine work, inoculated remts	
	2nd		Routine work, inoculated remts	
	3rd		Inspected horses at Cilledy Camp. ENG 15 to dispatch to base	
	4th		Had 1 horse of 14th M.O.S. destroyed, and carcase to butcher	
	5th		Routine work, inoculated remts. Sent off monthly Return of accounts for Jan. & Feb. to Irridental admin.	
	6th		Routine work	
	7th		Inspection 368 horses at Annual Collect'g for dispatch to base.	
	8th		Arranged for the dispatch of 1 cohorts of other ranks, 9/13th & 14th M.O.S. Surplus to Cadre to the 4 Vety Hospital Rolow	
	9th		2 other rank other ranks despatched to the 4 Vety Hosp. Calais. Inspected remts.	
	10th		Sent escort to NAMUR for 17721 Pte Holroyd who was granted leave to England on 1st of Feb. & failed to return	
	11th		Remanded Pte Holroyd for court-martial. Had summary of evidence taken	

M6945 Wt. W14422/M160 350,000 12/16 D.D. & L. Forms/C./2118/14.

(2) Volume 163. **WAR DIARY** 13th & 14th Army Form C. 2118.
April **INTELLIGENCE SUMMARY.** Mobile Vety Sections

Instructions regarding War Diaries and Intelligence Summaries are contained in F. S. Regs., Part II. and the Staff Manual respectively. Title pages will be prepared in manuscript.

(Erase heading not required.)

Place	Date	Hour	Summary of Events and Information	Remarks and references to Appendices
AMAY	12th		Routine work. Visited units	
"	13th		The Veterinarian inspected 25 dogs & 70 Mls 2 Mj 3.S.C.M.	
			Checked Stores of 14th MVS. Very bad	
"	14th		Completed instruct. for reference in Stores of 14th & 16th MVS. Visited units	
	15th		Routine work	
	16th		" Visited units	
	17th		Routine work	
	18th		Reconnoitred bridges to demobilize Sergt. Farrier R.A.V.C.	
	19th		Inspected forms of annual letting. Camp ENGIS	
	20th		Routine work	
	21st		Sergt. Farrier on one extra courses from demob'g when Routine work.	
	22M		Routine work	
ENGIS	23rd		Orders 8 13th & 14th M.V.SS. move to ENGIS	
AMAY	23rd		Chef Warner & Starling to 39 th MVS Vety. Sect. 1st Div. for m	
			14th MVS Vety Sept.	

(3) Volume 164

13th v/14 U
Mot Vily fochau

WAR DIARY
INTELLIGENCE SUMMARY
Army Form C. 2118.

Place	Date	Hour	Summary of Events and Information	Remarks and references to Appendices
EN CIS	25th		Sergt Joyser # Pte saunders 13th M.U.S. + Pte Hologed to 13th Cdn Bn for duty	
"	26th		Routine work	
"	27		"	
"	28		"	
"	29		"	
"	30		"	

JJMcC
ff. Capt R.C.R.
O.C. 13 M V/14 Ub Mol Very Sictors

WAR DIARY of 14th Mobile Veterinary Section. Army Form C. 2118.

or

INTELLIGENCE SUMMARY. MAY, 1919.

(Erase heading not required.)

Place	Date	Hour	Summary of Events and Information	Remarks and references to Appendices
	1919.			
ENGIS.	May 1st to 16th		No change.	
	17th		Captain J.J. MILLS, R.A.V.C. proceeded U.K. for service in India. Details of Section attached H.Q. 3rd Cavalry Division Cadre for administration.	
	18th to 31st.		No change.	

8/6/19.

[signature]
Lieutenant,
Camp Commandant,
3rd Cavalry Division H.Q. Cadre.